T0373745

Ha'ra

Home of the Vapra Clan and for many generations the seat of Gelfling power.

Grot

A cave-filled mountain range that is home to the Grottan Clan and Vliste-Staba, the Sanctuary Tree. Grot is also the ancestral homeland of the spiderlike Arathim.

The Endless Forest

A massive, eternal woodland area that covers more of Thra than any other named region. Gelfling of the Stonewood Clan live here, along with many other species.

The Spriton Plains

Forest and agricultural land inhabited by the Spriton Clan.

The Valley of the Mystics

An isolated stone valley where the urRu spent the Age of Division.

BESTIARY

BESTIARY

The Definitive Guide to the Creatures of Thra

Foreword by

Brian and Wendy Froud

Written by | Illustrated by

Adam Cesare | Iris Compiet

THE JIM HENSON COMPANY

Titan BOOKS

LONDON

AN INSIGHT EDITIONS BOOK

CONTENTS

FOREWORD
BY BRIAN AND WENDY FROUD

Originally, the world of The Dark Crystal, as imagined by Jim Henson, was called Mythra. The name reflected the resonant stories told and retold of ancient civilizations populated by fabled beings. The word Mythra, we felt, was too similar to Mithras, a real ancient religion, and so it was shortened to Thra.

The essential truth of Thra was that of a sentient world; all things—creatures, landscapes, plants—were connected, and all were imbued with life, personality, and mutual purpose. No one thing had dominion over another, and all moved in harmony and purpose with each other.

When we, Jim's team, were designing and building the creatures and landscape forms of Thra, they came to embody the various mystical forces of Jim's imaginal world.

The creative skills of puppet creators, costumiers, and set designers and builders all blended to express an emotional and spiritual reality. The mundane physicality of rubber and metal, glue, fabric, paint, and plaster were transcended to reveal an astonishing world as rich and strange as any expressed before.

It was a privilege to be invited into Jim's imaginative mind. He encouraged us to be fully part of it—to wonder at the beauty of an inner world that reflected the possibilities of an open and loving view of our own troubled planet.

As the years pass since the inception of the world of The Dark Crystal, more and more aspects of that world have been revealed via novels, graphic novels, and a new, lavish television series. Now, in this incredibly comprehensive bestiary, we can delight in the beautiful evocations of the wild and sometimes really wild denizens of Thra. Here in these pages, the luminous and thoughtful art of Iris Compiet illustrates the incredibly complex and mysterious world of Thra, and, by doing so, takes us ever farther toward the inner spirit of Jim Henson's vision. Each sentient being, whether from the tiniest and seemingly most insignificant clumps of vegetation, to the most imposing of creatures, such as the Skeksis, Mystics, and Lore, is lovingly portrayed in both word and picture. Each Gelfling clan is explored and documented in detail, and the relationship between the Skeksis and Mystics is beautifully explained.

This is the perfect book for anyone wishing to navigate, explore, and investigate the multifaceted, multilayered, and ever-expanding world that is Thra.

Brian Froud   Wendy Froud

THE WORLD OF THRA

The varied regions of Thra are full of creatures that graze, soar, hop, burrow, and slither. The planet teems with plant and animal life.

But to understand life on Thra is to understand the planet itself—all are one under Thra's three suns, and the boundaries between plant and animal life are remarkably fluid.

In the beginning, Thra was a primitive planet. That is, until the Crystal, Thra's living heart, conjured forth a protector—a voice—for the trees, stones, water, and animals of Thra. So entered Mother Aughra, the living embodiment of the planet as well as its spiritual guardian.

Aughra sees all the creatures of Thra as her children, from the playful Podlings to the deadly Gobbles. While she watches over and protects all life on the planet, Aughra does have favored children—the Gelfling.

An inherently gentle race who have always strived to live in harmony with the natural world, the Gelfling developed their language, culture, and ethics under Aughra's guidance. Over the trine, as the Gelfling became more independent, Aughra allowed her attention to stray to the wider cosmos, a preoccupation that would have devastating consequences for Thra.

Thra's surface features a large central landmass surrounded by ocean. Over millennia of change, this landmass has been naturally divided into several regions, named by the Gelfling tribes that have explored and settled these areas.

Located somewhere in the vastness of the universe, Thra orbits around its three suns—the largest of these is the Great Sun, the smallest the Dying Sun, and the Rose Sun the most colorful. Beneath its surface, Thra also houses the Mother Sun, a stellar anomaly that hangs over the underground realm of Mithra.

Above the Mother Sun, on Thra's surface, the Crystal hovers in a shaft of light and air within the Castle of the Crystal. The Crystal connects all life on Thra, from the lowliest of Lefar Worms to the most majestic of Crystal Skimmers. Because of this link, the Crystal's health impacts the well-being of every creature on Thra. If it is damaged or corrupted, the planet suffers, and death and sickness spreads among its inhabitants.

Every thousand trine, Thra's suns align in what is called a Great Conjunction. When the light of these aligned suns shines onto the Crystal, the power generated can have world-changing effects on Thra.

The First Great Conjunction delivered an alien race, the urSkeks, to the planet, bringing an end to what is now known as the Age of Innocence. The benign urSkeks brought scientific learning and technological advancement to the Gelfling and gave Aughra awareness of the wider universe. During this Age of Harmony, the urSkeks carved the Castle of the Crystal from the mountain that housed Thra's beating heart. During this period, the Crystal was clear and bright in color, in tune with the life-forms of Thra. But soon, it would become tarnished by corruption.

As the Second Great Conjunction approached, the urSkeks believed they could use the immense power generated by this astrological event to purify themselves of what they saw as their inherent imperfections. During the subsequent ceremony, the urSkeks were split into two distinct beings: the Skeksis and the urRu (also known as the Mystics). The Crystal cracked and darkened, turning purple, as the castle around it became the domain of the cruel Skeksis, with the peaceful urRu fleeing into exile.

The following thousand trine became known as the Age of Division. Calling themselves the Lords of the Crystal, the Skeksis ruled over the Gelfling, posing as kindly benefactors. With Aughra locked away in her observatory, her

consciousness exploring the universe, the Skeksis pillaged the natural world, slaughtering its animals in huge numbers and subjugating many of its sentient species.

By the last hundred trine of the Age of Division, the Skeksis had total dominion over the planet, but even that wasn't enough. They wanted eternal life.

Twisting the Crystal into a tool of destruction, the Skeksis began using the heart of Thra to artificially extend their own lives, draining first the world itself and then the Gelflings' life essence. This unnatural abuse of the Crystal accelerated the Darkening, a destructive force that threatened to turn Thra into a lifeless wasteland. After uncovering the Skeksis' malevolent plans, the seven Gelfling clans united against their masters during an epoch known as the Age of Resistance.

Following much tragedy, the Third Great Conjunction saw the last surviving Gelfling heroes, Jen and Kira, reform the Crystal, overcoming the evil Skeksis to rejoin the two halves of the urSkeks and heal the world. This final conjunction ushered in the Age of Power.

Though much of the natural world had been decimated by the Darkening, all was not lost. The Age of Power saw the surviving creatures of Thra bounce back from the edge of extinction, the planet once again becoming lush and verdant.

While not all creatures of Thra are mighty like Landstriders, beautiful like Unamoths, or make loyal companions like Fizzgigs, all are worthy of our fascination, respect, and further study. Some of these creatures come from another world, some another time. Some sadly no longer exist, but all have something to teach us about our relationship to this wider world of wonders.

THE GELFLING

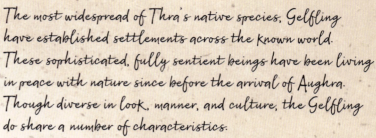

The most widespread of Thra's native species, Gelfling have established settlements across the known world. These sophisticated, fully sentient beings have been living in peace with nature since before the arrival of Aughra. Though diverse in look, manner, and culture, the Gelfling do share a number of characteristics.

Gelfling are bipedal and have slender features, lithe limbs, and delicate, four-fingered hands. Unlike the males, female Gelfling have a set of light, translucent wings that allow them to fly and glide.

The Gelfling are known to dreamfast, a practice that enables them to meld their spiritual consciousness. During this communion, two or more Gelfling can pass memories back and forth to one another. While there are limits to dreamfasting—for example, one Gelfling cannot pass on the memories of another—this ability has been a great asset to both learning and storytelling throughout Gelfling history.

With practice and training, Gelfling can also produce dreametchings. Similar to written language, dreametchings are messages left on objects or surfaces. Gelfling can commune with these dreametchings, receiving the thought or memory imprinted there.

Gelfling are social creatures. In the early days of Thra, they adopted a tribal culture that ensured the survival and longevity of their species. Under the teaching and protection of Aughra, these early Gelfling tribes gained knowledge of the natural world and began to develop a more complex, unified culture.

Upon their arrival, the Skeksis codified Gelfling culture into seven distinct clans, a tactic to secretly sow division. Gelfling clans are matriarchal—each clan headed by an appointed female leader known as a Maudra. The Skeksis chose their most favored clan and promoted its leader to the position of All-Maudra, ruler of all Gelfling throughout Thra.

GELFLING CLANS

VAPRA

The Vapra live high in the snow-topped cliffs overlooking the Silver Sea. They are creatures of altitude, air, and lightness. Fair in hair and complexion, the Vapra's appearance allows them to disappear among the snowdrifts of their mountain home—a skill that has led many Vapra to boast that their clan are masters of disguise.

Often considered haughty by their fellow Gelfling. Vapra believe that their culture is statelier and more refined than that of the other six clans. This sense of superiority is no doubt rooted in the fact that for almost a thousand trine after the arrival of the Skeksis, most All-Maudra were Vapran. This political dominance, a result of the Skeksis patronage, meant that for long stretches, the Vapran capital of Ha'rar served as the de facto capital for Gelfling society.

Spriton

Earthy and simple, the Spriton are a farming clan. They are equally at home tending rolling plains of farmland and raising beasts of burden like Landstriders or Mounders in their forest capital, Sami Thicket, which is landlocked in the center of Thra. Through trade, the industrious Spriton keep many of the other clans clothed and fed. Though they are humble, rugged, and independent, many Spriton are also artisans, able to produce not only crops and livestock but works of great beauty such as sublime pottery and dress finery.

Dark haired, the Spriton have calloused hands and sun-worn skin. Most spend their lives working the land and can often be seen wearing simple clothing in sedate earth tones that match their pastoral environment.

Though generally peaceful, the Spriton have been known to engage in disputes with their neighbors, the Stonewood Clan. But these spats rarely rise above name-calling and rumormongering.

STONEWOOD

Residing in the Endless Forest, the Stonewood's proximity to the Castle of the Crystal led them to find employment as armored guards for the Skeksis during the time of the Second Great Conjunction. Over time, they came to compose the bulk of the Skeksis' military might and fought for their masters during the Arathim rebellion, a series of battles against a race of sentient arachnids despised by the Skeksis. Honorable warriors, the Stonewood were also the first of the Gelfling to officially stand against their former lords during the Age of Resistance, once it was revealed that the Skeksis were draining the Gelfling to consume their essence. The Stonewood capital is Stone-in-the-Wood, site of the famed first uprising against the Skeksis.

Despite their physical strength and martial prowess, Stonewood are known to be tranquil and in tune with the natural world. The Endless Forest is the most biologically diverse region of Thra, and the clan respect and honor the many creatures with which they share their home. Regardless of their role within the clan or station within society, Stonewood prefer to wear armor rather than regular civilian clothing or luxurious linens and silks.

While the Stonewood are warriors first and foremost, at the end of each military campaign, they place their weapons in a giant forge called the Crucible. This periodic disarmament is a symbolic gesture by the Stonewood meant to indicate that they have set aside violence and aggression in order to focus on healing—a practice espoused by the proverb "The hand that holds the blade cannot help the fallen to their feet."

SIFA

The Sifa have spent many ages sailing the oceans of Thra. In fact, they feel so at home on the water that some Gelfling say they have more in common with the creatures of the Silver Sea than with their land-dwelling relatives. Due to their nomadic, fragmented history, there is no one central Sifan culture. As a result, communities found on individual Sifan ships and fleets can vary wildly in their customs and cultural practices.

Because their seabound way of life is dangerous, the Sifa look to mystical wards and symbols for protection. Even their children have a working understanding of magic and symbology. Many Gelfling from other clans view the Sifa's preoccupation with the unknown and soothsaying as unhealthy superstitions.

Sifan crews often recruit Gelfling who have either left their birth clan or been forced out. Because of their frequent acceptance of outcasts, they are one of the most diverse clans both physically and in terms of their cultural outlook. However, the decentralized, free-roaming nature of Sifan society has led to a great deal of distrust from other clans, particularly as rogue Sifa have been known to resort to piracy and—in extremely isolated cases—slavery.

DRENCHEN

No Gelfling is as physically strong—or as damp—as a Drenchen. Making their home deep in the Swamp of Sog, the Drenchen are geographically isolated from the rest of Thra.

Biologically distinct from other Gelfling, Drenchen have greenish-gold hair and skin. This tint is attributed to a combination of diet (lichens and tadpoles) and algae buildup (a result of being submerged in swamp water for most of their days). They also keep their hair in distinctive braided locks.

Drenchen are the only Gelfling that have developed gills for breathing under water—and females of the species have unusually thick wings more suited to swimming than flight.

At the center of their territory is an ancient tree, the Great Smerth, which serves as the Drenchen capital.

GROTTAN

Living in the caves beneath the mountains of Grot, the Grottan's main source of light is the soft glow of bioluminescent moss—their murky environment endowing them with distinctive features including pale green skin, large black eyes, and elongated ears.

The Grottan share their home with a large number of creatures and have successfully tamed many of these animal neighbors, including Nurlocs and Hollerbats. To protect themselves from more unruly creatures, they utilize a number of nonlethal methods of deterrence, including smoke bombs.

Because the ecosystem of Grot is incredibly insular, the Grottan Clan monitor the roots of Vliste-Staba, the Sanctuary Tree that sits atop their mountain range, for signs of potential threats from the outside world.

The Grottan are fiercely proud of their subterranean lifestyle and regard the other six clans with skepticism. Most Grottan spend the entirety of their lives in their caves and never once venture overground.

DOUSAN

The nomadic Dousan are the most enigmatic of all Gelfling clans. Clad in ritual face paint and elaborate charms that represent their beliefs in sacred geometry, the Dousan live in the barren wilds of the Crystal Desert. Many Dousan travel the desert on the back of Crystal Skimmers, a species of enormous flying creatures with which they have developed a symbiotic relationship. While many Dousan would not claim they have a home or a capital city, their travels always lead them back to Oszah-Staba—also known as the Wellspring Tree—a verdant desert oasis where Dousan can meet and trade.

Some Gelfling fear the Dousan, believing that they worship death. However, the Dousan's spirituality is far more nuanced. They hold sacred the circular process by which life ends in death but begins again through Thra's lush bounty. For a Dousan, death is not the end, nor is it cause for fear or sorrow. For many Dousan, becoming comfortable with death is a lifelong spiritual pursuit.

Dousan have many esoteric rituals that are viewed with trepidation by Gelfling from other clans. Some require Dousan shamans to ingest urdrupes, hallucinogenic berries that allow them to commune with Thra and glimpse the future, albeit briefly and imperfectly. Though somewhat odd, these Dousan rituals help the clan face the harshness of life in the Crystal Desert, foreseeing approaching dangers and illuminating the path to precious resources.

THE SKEKSIS AND THE MYSTICS

urSKEKS

Ethereal, tall, and fantastically powerful, the urSkeks are an alien race from the farthest reaches of the cosmos. During the First Great Conjunction, eighteen representatives of their species found themselves stranded on Thra, pushed out of their home world for reasons they have never revealed in full. What is known is that the urSkeks' planet, like Thra, also had a crystal at its heart, and tampering with it led to their exile.

By sharing their wisdom and technological advancements with Aughra and the Gelfling, these eighteen urSkeks were able to drastically advance life on Thra. Most notably, they used their immense psychic and telekinetic abilities to reshape parts of the world and construct the Castle of the Crystal. But even as they tried to wield their immense powers in a noble manner, the urSkeks could not escape the darkness within themselves.

During the Second Great Conjunction, the urSkeks' yearning to return to their home planet led them to take actions that triggered a catastrophic event. Upon stepping into the combined light of the suns, the urSkeks were divided into two separate species: the wise and altruistic urRu and the clutching, greedy Skeksis. The two species were mostly autonomous, but not entirely. If an urRu suffered an injury, its Skeksis counterpart would feel it—and no one half could live if the other died. Though they are largely opposite in appearance and demeanor, the urRu and Skeksis do have some physiological similarities—both have four arms along with tails that they use for balance.

Moments after the Great Division, the furious Skeksis cracked the crystal, corrupting its power for the next thousand trine and starting a chain of events that would bring Thra to the brink of destruction.

Of the eighteen Skesis and urRu created by the Second Great Conjunction, only eight of each species would survive another thousand trine to be rejoined when the Crystal was healed.

SKEKSO THE EMPEROR

Callous, ruthless, and calculating, skekSo was the first Skeksis to claim the title of Emperor, his reign lasting nearly a thousand trine. A charismatic leader, skekSo was able to maintain his supremacy by deftly playing his would-be rivals against one another. It was under his direction that skekTek the Scientist was tasked with harnessing the power of the Dark Crystal to extend Skeksis' life indefinitely. Late in the Age of Division, skekSo came to understand the ramifications of this exploitation. Using the Crystal to drain the life from the creatures of Thra had created a destructive energy called the Darkening. Arrogant and megalomaniacal, skekSo wrongly believed he could control this blighted dark energy, and though it took many trine, it was this early exposure to the Darkening that precipitated his eventual death.

URSU THE MASTER

urSu was the wise and melancholy leader of the Mystics. Throughout most of the Age of Division, urSu maintained that the urRu should not intervene in the political and cultural clashes of Thra, since the urSkeks, and therefore the Mystics themselves, were not of Thra. urSu changed his position after witnessing the Skeksis subjugate and exterminate several native species. urSu adopted Jen, one of the last Gelfling left alive, after he was orphaned in a raid carried out by the Skeksis' beetle-like soldiers, the Garthim. urSu kept Jen safe, preparing him for the day when he would leave their home in the Valley of the Mystics to begin a quest that would bring an end to Skeksis rule.

SKEKZOK THE RITUAL MASTER

Pompous, erudite, and fastidious, skekZok was charged with inventing, planning, and officiating the Skeksis' many ceremonies and religious rituals. Not only was skekZok the court's high priest, he was also skekSo's most trusted adviser and kept a rookery of Crystal Bats that he used to clandestinely gather information for his master. skekZok hid his cruelty under a veneer of civility and etiquette, but his penchant for torture and execution made him one of the most diabolical Skeksis.

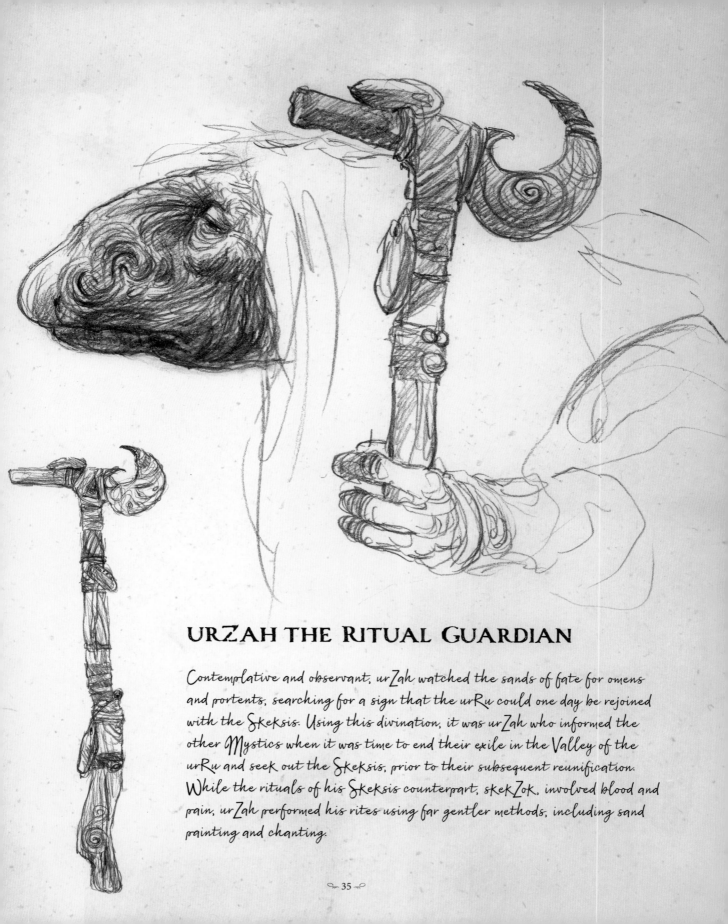

URZAH THE RITUAL GUARDIAN

Contemplative and observant, urZah watched the sands of fate for omens and portents, searching for a sign that the urRu could one day be rejoined with the Skeksis. Using this divination, it was urZah who informed the other Mystics when it was time to end their exile in the Valley of the urRu and seek out the Skeksis, prior to their subsequent reunification. While the rituals of his Skeksis counterpart, skekZok, involved blood and pain, urZah performed his rites using far gentler methods, including sand painting and chanting.

skekSil the Chamberlain

Obsequious and conniving, skekSil was a master of persuasion and two-faced politicking. For much of skekSo's reign, skekSil served as the Emperor's trusted advisor, a comfortable position that required skekSil to maintain a number of uneasy alliances with his fellow Skeksis. skekSil possessed an unusually strong understanding of others' motivations and desires, making him a master manipulator who excelled at sowing doubt in the minds of his peers and subordinates. Although he rarely felt empathy and compassion, he was a master at mimicking both. In many ways, his boundless duplicity made skekSil the most dangerous of all the Skeksis.

URSOL THE CHANTER

A gentle soul, yet more opinionated than
the other Mystics, urSol could speak
in a tremulous whisper or raise his chants
to be heard beyond the Valley of the urRu.
While urSol's Skeksis counterpart used his voice
to make the world a worse place, urSol chose to enrich Thra with song.
urSol had such a powerful command of his voice that he was able to
inspire the natural world to vibrate and sing along with him in harmony.

SKEKVAR THE GENERAL

skekVar was the original military leader of the Skeksis. For more than eight hundred trine, he ran dozens of successful campaigns against both armed and unarmed races: quashing the Arathim, inciting war when the subterranean Makraks rose to the surface, and annihilating a peaceful race known as the Gruenaks. Even though he possessed moderate skills as a tactician, skekVar frequently undercut his own successes because of his impatience and temper. While he was one of the most physically powerful Skeksis, his overconfidence finally got the better of him when he underestimated the combat prowess of the Gelfling hero Rian. Badly injured in the duel, skekVar was subsequently betrayed and murdered by skekSil as revenge for the many humiliations he had suffered at the hands of the hot-headed General.

urMa the Peacemaker

One of the few urRu who broke from urSu the Master's centuries-long doctrine of not intervening in the conflicts of Thra, urMa was always willing to arbitrate, defusing situations before squabbles turned into wars. He was not blind to the Skeksis' capacity for duplicity and evil, but he did understand that they could be reasoned with, to an extent. Though he died at the same time skekVar was killed, it's unlikely that even this careful negotiator would have been able to stem the violence that broke out toward the end of the Age of Division.

SKEKUNG THE GARTHIM MASTER

Physically powerful and ambitious, skekUng knew what it took to seize power and keep it. After the death of skekVar, skekUng became the new Skeksis General, inventing the title of Garthim Master for himself. A keen military tactician, skekUng used his Garthim soldiers to root out surviving pockets of Gelfling resistance, taking prisoners who would be harvested for their essence. skekUng reinforced his armor using the carapaces of Garthim soldiers, cementing his position as one of the most physically fearsome Skeksis. skekUng would later defeat skekSil in a ritualistic battle known as the Trial by Stone, replacing skekSo as the second Skeksis Emperor. His reign was brief.

URIM THE HEALER

Nurturing and hopeful, urIm believed that there was no hurt that need go untreated. Not only an expert in using medicines, poultices, and acupuncture to heal the body, urIm also salved the soul through more esoteric medicines like wind dancing and urRu throat singing. When urSu the Master died, urIm assumed leadership of the Mystics and led their pilgrimage to the Castle of the Crystal where they would be rejoined with their dark halves.

SKEKTEK THE SCIENTIST

Intelligent, learned, and vicious, skekTek used his intuitive understanding of science and technology to commit heinous atrocities—crimes he often referred to as mere "experiments." Even though his comrades often benefited from his discoveries, skekTek always ranked lowest in the Skeksis pecking order and was a frequent target for bullying. Losing an eye through corporal punishment only served to further stoke skekTek's inferiority complex. Despite his lowly status, skekTek has had more of a negative impact on Thra than any other single being. It was skekTek who invented the process for draining Gelfling of their essence, further polluting the Crystal and accelerating the Darkening. He also created the terrifying Garthim, an act of cold-blooded malevolence that led to many trine of suffering for the Gelfling.

urTih the Alchemist

An ethical master of invention, urTih was patient and humble, knowing that his works should never challenge the beauty and power of the natural world. Sadly, this urRu's life was tragic. Whenever skekTek was beaten, bullied, or maimed by the other Skeksis, urTih would endure the same injury. As a result, over the course of urTih's life, he lost an arm, a leg, and an eye. urTih disappeared from Thra when skekTek was killed near the end of Jen and Kira's quest to heal the Crystal.

SKEKAYUK THE GOURMAND

skekAyuk was relatively benign compared with his fellow Skeksis—not because he was morally superior but because his rapacious overeating left him little time to indulge in evil. At the beginning of the Age of Division, skekAyuk was a skilled cook with a refined palate, but by the end of that period, he had lost the knack for creation and only consumed, becoming bloated and complacent. But skekAyuk's greatest sin was not his gluttony, it was his failure to warn the other Skeksis that their consumption of Gelfling essence would lead to Thra's destruction, even though he was one of the first to recognize its dangers.

urAmaj the Cook

Like his darker half, urAmaj drew great pleasure from food, but his enthusiasm was for meal preparation rather than endless eating. When creating dishes for his Mystic brethren, urAmaj prized texture and flavor, working with his great friend urNol the Herbalist to make sure the meals were perfectly spiced and appropriately wholesome. Like most Mystics, urAmaj was never in much of a rush, but fortunately his dishes were best consumed cold.

SKEKNA THE SLAVE MASTER

Tasked with enslaving some of Thra's most docile races—including the Podlings and the now-extinct Gruenaks—skekNa kept to the shadows while his fellow Skeksis were pretending to be the Gelflings' benefactors. Late in the Age of Division, as relations soured between the Gelfling and Skeksis, skekNa was no longer required to hide his cruelty and became a key figure in rounding up the Gelfling population so they could be drained of their essence.

Not as physically imposing as some of the other Skeksis, he became adept at exerting his power over those weaker than him, beings in no position to fight back.

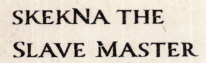

In the days before the Age of Resistance, skekNa fell afoul of his Emperor after committing several acts of brutality that risked exposing the true nature of the Skeksis. Sentenced to lose his hand, skekNa opted to wear a jagged metal hook in its place, refusing skekTek's offer to build him a mechanical prosthesis. skekNa would also lose an eye for a similar offense.

urNol the Herbalist

Best friend to urAmaj the Cook, urNol kept a garden
of herbs in the Valley of the Mystics. Especially
unhurried, even for a Mystic, he chose to see periods
of introspection or reflection as opportunities for his crops
to bloom or his jars of tinctures to ferment. Though urNol did
not incur the same level of injury as urTih did throughout his life,
like skekNa he was missing an eye, and one of his hands was split down
the middle. urNol saw this injury as an asset, rather than an impediment,
believing it gave him improved dexterity while gathering herbs.

SKEKOK THE SCROLL KEEPER

A posing, preening pseudo-intellectual, skekOk was in charge of recording Skeksis history and laws. Manipulative and deceitful to the point of compulsion, skekOk frequently falsified historical accounts to suit his own needs and whims. He was able to successfully enforce many contradictory interpretations of his own laws because the other Skeksis found skekOk so tiresome that they went out of their way to avoid talking to him. Even the row of spectacles running down his beak were just a pantomime—although skekOk was granted perfect vision by the Gelfling essence he consumed, he kept wearing the spectacles to further boost his image as a serious academic.

URAC THE SCRIBE

While skekOk filled reams of parchment with lies and fabrications, his urRu counterpart, urAc, was preoccupied with recording truth, his writings often bordering on works of art—impressionistic and interpretive. urAc would sit with his compatriots for long hours, listening to their stories and memories and later trying to capture their meaning in multiple mediums, not only writing on scrolls but also weaving tapestries and sculpting with hammer and chisel. urAc was always in search of a new way to impart universal truths, even if his definition of truth was symbolic rather than strictly factual.

SKEKSHOD THE TREASURER

Weighed down by fine silks and gemstones, skekShod was in charge of accounting for the Skeksis' accrued riches. Unpopular among his fellow Skeksis, skekShod was deemed so weak and ineffectual that, even after two unsuccessful attempts at dethroning skekSo, he was spared from torture. skekShod claimed that he would move the Gelfling away from a barter economy and introduce standard denominations, but he proved too lazy to follow through on his promises. Instead, he spent his time counting his trinkets and glistening stones while the Gelfling languished.

urYod the Numerologist

urYod counted. What urYod counted was sometimes a mystery even to himself—that is, until he completed the calculations on his great abacus. He was a living calendar and a beacon of accuracy in an inaccurate world, keeping track of the rotations of Thra's nearby stars and planets and the passage of time across many trine. Careful and considerate, urYod went about his work quietly, synthesizing the obscure signs, portents, and omens observed by the urRu into digestible pieces of information that could be shared with the group.

SKEKEKT THE ORNAMENTALIST

The designer of the Skeksis' gaudy garments, skekEkt crafted outfits for his cronies that reflected the wearers' personalities and occupations. Vain and conceited, skekEkt was undeniably a skilled tailor but always kept the best pieces for himself. skekEkt understood that fashion came at a price, and none was too high if it meant looking good. If a rare bird needed to be plucked to provide a fringe for his latest dress design, then why not kill two? If skekEkt's makeup proved poisonous to the Podling slaves forced to apply it? Then the castle would need some new slaves.

urUtt the Weaver

The ceremonial robes worn by the Mystics were carefully prepared by urUtt. More than simple clothing, each told a story about the wearer, capturing their spirit and honoring their long life on Thra. Whenever the Mystics' clothes needed mending, urUtt would prepare his weave and loom, adding new flourishes to each design to reflect the ever-changing nature of the wearer. One of the most empathic and caring of the Mystics, urUtt always prioritized the clothes of others, sometimes allowing his own robes to fall into disrepair while he worked for the benefit of his fellow Mystics.

SKEKLACH
THE COLLECTOR

Despite being responsible for sourcing the
Skeksis' vast wealth, skekLach was never satisfied.
During the Age of Division, skekLach oversaw
tithing, a form of taxation that required Gelfling
from all over Thra to provide the Skeksis with
whatever riches they had managed to scrape
together. skekLach was so greedy and demanding
during tithing ceremonies that Gelfling dreaded her
attendance. Pessimistic and neurotic, skekLach started to suffer
from pustules during the height of the Skeksis power—these later became
swollen boils that developed into weeping ulcerative sores. As skekLach's
skin complaints worsened, she became even colder and more vindictive.
skekLach was killed at the Battle of Stone-in-the-Wood, struck by a
concentrated beam channeling the power of the Darkening. Following the
Collector's death, the Treasurer soon stepped in to fill her role.

URSEN THE MONK

Little is known about urSen the Monk, but that alone demonstrates the unassuming nature of his life. Shortly after the urRu exiled themselves to the Valley of the Mystics, urSen sought further seclusion, moving to a cave on the region's outskirts. According to urSol the Chanter, it was possible that urSen had witnessed a premonition of his own death and spent the last hundred trine of his life quietly contemplating his impending fate.

SKEKMAL THE HUNTER

The Skeksis were afraid of very few things, and one of those things was skekMal the Hunter. Wearing an outfit assembled from the bones of past kills, he was considered fearsome and unpredictable, even by his brethren. There was no quarry too large or too dangerous for skekMal, an unparalleled warrior and the most cunning tracker on Thra. While he was treated as an outcast by his brethren, they nevertheless understood the Hunter's usefulness, even installing a giant horn atop the Castle of the Crystal to call him home in times of need. While skekMal was a terrifying foe, he was also the only Skeksis who possessed a code of honor—relishing a fair fight, he lived to hunt worthy prey. skekMal met his end not at the hands of his enemies, but through the bravery of his urRu counterpart.

URVA THE ARCHER

Much like his dark half, urVa was an outsider, even among his fellow Mystics. Athletic and quick-witted, urVa often left the Valley of the Mystics to roam Thra. A master of both hand-to-hand combat and archery, urVa made a solemn oath to only take a life when absolutely necessary. urVa had a profound respect for nature and spent most of his days adventuring in the Endless Forest and surrounding areas. Possessing forestry and tracking skills that equaled those of skekMal, urVa kept tabs on his other half. His final act was to put an end to his bloodthirsty counterpart by taking his own life.

SKEKGRA THE CONQUEROR/HERETIC

skekGra's existence proves that no life-form is irredeemable. Early in the Age of Division, skekGra the Conqueror traveled the unexplored regions of Thra, subjugating all he found. But in later trine, he renounced his conqueror ways, only to be labeled the Heretic by his fellow Skeksis. skekGra's moral awakening came about slowly, starting as a secret sympathy toward the Mystics and culminating in a great vision, triggered by the consumption of urdrupe berries. In this vision, skekGra foresaw the ruination of Thra by the Skeksis and realized that the only way to prevent this catastrophe was for his corrupt race to be reunited with their better halves. Although during his early years skekGra was skilled only in war, once befriending urGoh, his Mystic counterpart, he developed a number of other hobbies, including mushroom farming, playwriting, puppetry, and pyrotechnics. To better attune his mind to the vibrations of the Crystal, skekGra installed a metal spike in his head, and, as penance for his past sins, he bound one set of arms behind his back.

URGOH THE WANDERER

After wandering the hills and forests of Thra for many trine, urGoh was reunited with skekGra and finally found purpose working with his counterpart to find a way to reunite as one being. Artistic, outgoing, and friendly, urGoh had a good sense of humor and an even better singing voice. He was also a fast talker—at least by Mystic standards. Alongside skekGra, urGoh traveled to Mithra, beneath Thra's surface, to forge the Dual Glaive, a mighty weapon that could be used to defeat the Skeksis. They also built and programmed Lore, a friendly machine that would assist their allies in the fight to save Thra. Although they certainly had their differences, skekGra and urGoh were instrumental in setting the Gelfling on the path to healing the Crystal and rejoining the Skeksis with the urRu.

PROTECTORS OF THRA

AUGHRA

Summoned forth as nature's protector, Mother Aughra unifies all life on Thra. As biologically anomalous as she is aloof and wise, there is no life-form like Aughra, and she watches over all the creatures of Thra.

    Aughra is neither plant nor animal—she is all of Thra in one being. Her veins flow with sap and her feet and hands were once roots that, at birth, connected her to the dirt. She has curved horns and three eyes—the removable middle eye capable of remote viewing and even peering into the future. Behind these eyes is a mind that has grown weary under the burden of a cosmos' worth of knowledge. At times cantankerous, she never stops caring for her world and its many species and is willing to sacrifice everything to protect them.

Even though she is the most powerful being on Thra, Aughra is not infallible, and like the Gelfling, she was initially unaware of the Skefksis' treachery. Using her precognitive powers, she foresaw the coming of the urSkeks but not the ruination their division would bring. Believing that the Skeksis were trustworthy custodians of Thra, she retreated to her hilltop orrery and spent many trine exploring the stars through astral projection. The Skeksis seized on her absence to subjugate the other races of Thra, unleashing the Darkening in the process.

    Awakening to a world in turmoil, Aughra immediately embarked on a quest to set things right.

RAUNIP

Well before the arrival of the urSkeks, a goopy, amorphous alien life-form crashed to Thra's surface inside a meteorite. Mother Aughra, fascinated with this organic material from the stars, took it and shaped it in her own image, naming the new being Raunip.

While many of the species on Thra consider themselves Aughra's children, only Raunip could claim to be her son. Friendly but mischievous, Raunip is shorter than his mother with slender limbs, long hooked fingers, and a puffball mane that surrounds his mismatched eyes.

During the Age of Harmony, Raunip was one of the few beings to become skeptical of the urSkeks, questioning the aliens' intentions toward Thra. His suspicions were ignored by his mother, who had grown increasingly distracted by the universe beyond Thra. Raunip saw the darkness at the heart of the urSkeks, and through his mischievous actions, he was instrumental in their division into the Skeksis and urRu.

LORE

Based on an antiquated piece of urSkek engineering
and constructed by skekGra and urGoh to help the Gelfling put
an end to Skeksis rule, Lore is a difficult creature to classify. His
body comprises several stacked stones carved with dreametchings,
held together by magic. While Lore was programmed for a specific
purpose, he is not a mindless automaton. Once he has
imprinted on a Gelfling, Lore becomes a peerless
bodyguard and companion. Not constrained by
the limits of flesh and blood, Lore can climb,
fight, and run with endless stamina. What
Lore lacks in dexterity and subtlety, he makes
up for in loyalty and strength. Lore is also
able to rearrange the configuration of his
body, allowing him mobility that belies his
considerable size.

PODLING

Podlings are lively, bipedal creatures that live in tight-knit communities. Their appearance can vary, but generally they have small beady eyes, prominent smiles, and rounded potato-like features.

Short and jovial, Podlings do not have room in their lives for sadness and introspection—or baths, for that matter. They are too busy planting crops, communing with their animal friends, and building the rudimentary musical instruments that they use to celebrate life itself.

Podlings have no organized political or religious structures in their society, but they do have a practice of naming an older, venerated Podling as Chief. They call this informal leader "The Father" and will consult with him in times of trouble.

Instinctively able to communicate with a vast number of Thra's animal species, Podlings are masters of domestication. Swamp-dwelling Podlings collect milk from the amphibious Nebries, while Podlings that live near open fields shear horned, shaggy Mounders for their fur. Even the temperamental fanged fuzz balls known as Fizzgigs have a natural affinity for Podlings.

While Podlings are strictly vegetarian,
they do harvest Nebrie flesh and bone, but only
when the animals die of natural causes. With
reverence, the Podlings use
these found resources
to fashion
instruments and
clothing.

Podlings originated in the Endless Forest but, as the
ages progressed, they ranged farther afield. Gelfling
first encountered Podlings sometime during the
Age of Harmony and dubbed them Pod People
because of the large seedpods they fashion into
homes and wayhouses.

While most Podlings are content with simple lives full of music and fun, some have followed grander callings—for example, the Podling paladin Hup, a great hero instrumental in the resistance against the Skeksis all while armed with only a spoon!

67

CREATURES OF THRA

MAKRAK

Once a proud race of miners and engineers, the Makraks were driven to violence when they lost their underground home. While they can appear fearsome with their prehensile antenna, glowing yellow eyes, and thick, chitinous shells, they are largely misunderstood.

Subterranean creatures acclimated to the heat and pressure of living near Thra's core, the Makraks were forced aboveground by tectonic shifts early in the Age of Division. Thra's cold, moist surface was inhospitable for the creatures, and wracked with pain, they lashed out at any beings unfortunate enough to cross their paths.

Made militant by homelessness and constant
pain, the Makraks came to the brink of war with
the early Gelfling clans. Fortunately, Raunip,
with the help of the urRu, interceded and convinced
the Makraks to live in the Field of Fire, an area
of Thra inhospitable to Gelfling. Rehomed, the
Makraks were much more comfortable and the
conflict was defused. However, even though peace
reigned for hundreds of trine, Gelfling parents would
still tell naughty children that if they didn't
behave, the Makraks would take them away.

ARATHIM

The Arathim comprise a number of subspecies of sentient arachnids all linked in thought and purpose by one hive mind. One of Thra's oldest races, they called the caves of Grot their ancestral homeland well before the formation of the Grottan Clan. Fiercely independent and oft-embattled, the Arathim became one of the first victims of the Skeksis' rise to power when they refused to serve as a military force for the self-appointed Lords of the Crystal. As punishment, the Skeksis drove them from Grot and gifted their caves to the Gelfling.

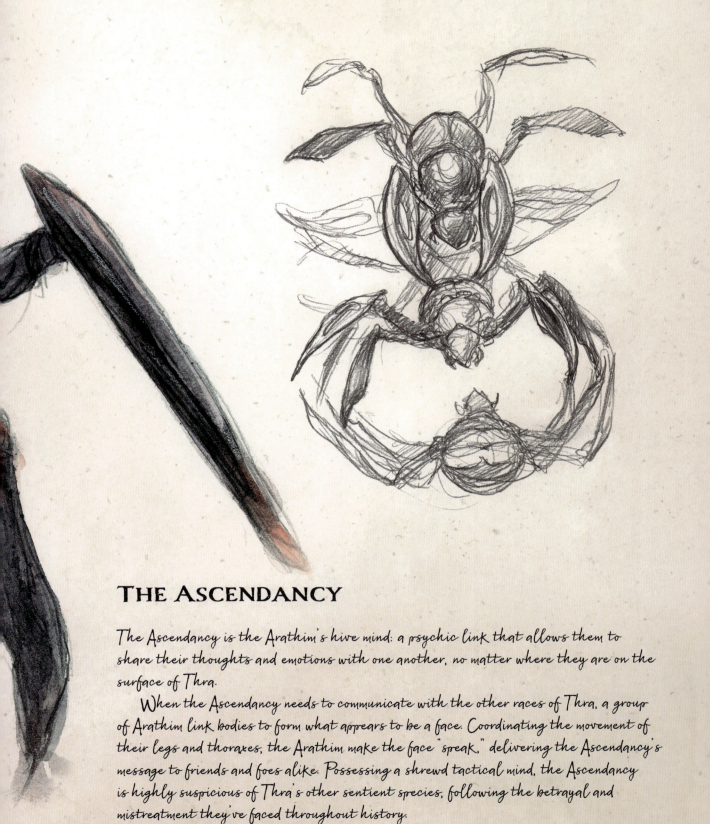

THE ASCENDANCY

The Ascendancy is the Arathim's hive mind: a psychic link that allows them to share their thoughts and emotions with one another, no matter where they are on the surface of Thra.

When the Ascendancy needs to communicate with the other races of Thra, a group of Arathim link bodies to form what appears to be a face. Coordinating the movement of their legs and thoraxes, the Arathim make the face "speak," delivering the Ascendancy's message to friends and foes alike. Possessing a shrewd tactical mind, the Ascendancy is highly suspicious of Thra's other sentient species, following the betrayal and mistreatment they've faced throughout history.

SPITTER

With six large limbs that can be used for stabbing and rending, Spitters are the warrior caste of Arathim society. There are two different kinds of Spitters. Poison Spitters expectorate caustic gobs of venom, blinding their prey before attacking. Silk Spitters produce thick ropes of unbreakable silk, which can be used in battle to subdue opponents. The Silk Spitters also utilize their secretions to build webs and other Arathim structures.

THREADER

A subspecies of Arathim capable of mind control,
Threaders forge a parasitic connection with their
hosts, attaching themselves to their victim's head,
where proximity to the brain increases the strength of
their psychic hold. Threaders are lightweight, with delicate
legs shaped like flower petals. Much smaller than other
Arathim—barely the span of a Gelfling hand—their flat,
thin limbs, when spread wide, allow them to glide short
distances and latch onto hosts. Once a connection is
complete, the victim's mind comes under the control
of the Arathim Ascendancy and they lose all sense
of self. If a Threader does not
disengage with its host in
less than a day, the
connection is
permanent—
removal will kill both
the host and the Threader.

GRUENAK

Possessing long arms, big mouths, gray skin, and flat faces, Gruenaks were one of Thra's most prominent sentient species during the Age of Harmony. With the arrival of the Skeksis at the beginning of the Age of Division, the Gruenaks found themselves facing a powerful enemy.

Ultimately, the Skeksis destroyed all but two Gruenaks. This unlucky pair was enslaved at the Castle of the Crystal and had their lips sewn shut so they could not share the cruelty of the Skeksis with others. skekTek took the corpse of the final Gruenak and spliced it with a fallen Arathim in order to engineer the first Garthim warrior.

Once renowned for their early technological advances, following their tragic extinction, Gruenak culture has been lost to the ravages of time.

GARTHIM

skekTek the Scientist gave life to the first Garthim warrior by combining Arathim and Gruenak corpses, using the power of the Dark Crystal to animate his creation. This ferocious, relentless creature was nothing short of an affront to the natural world.

Protected by large, obsidian armored plates, a Garthim warrior was roughly twice the height of an adult Gelfling. A single specimen could have upwards of twenty legs, grouped into two limbs. As the giant upright beetle-like creature scuttled across the ground, these groupings sometimes gave the illusion of bipedal motion.

Garthim were not creatures of stealth. When they moved, they rattled their carapace plates, clicking together their two large claws and the smaller sets of pincers that ran down the trunk of their torso. The sound of this motion was not unlike the rustling of seashells and soon became a noise that all of Thra learned to fear.

skekTek's army was unleashed on Thra to capture Podlings and Gelfling so their essence could be drained. This dark, violent period in the planet's history became known as the Garthim War and left the Gelfling on the brink of extinction, despite their brave attempts to fight back.

Following the Garthim War that left the Gelfling and Podling populations decimated, the hulking creatures were often relegated to guard duty in the hallways of the Castle of the Crystal. Unleashed to apprehend Gelfling heroes Jen and Kira at the end of the Age of Division, the Garthim were vanquished when Jen healed the Crystal, collapsing into inanimate piles of armor plating.

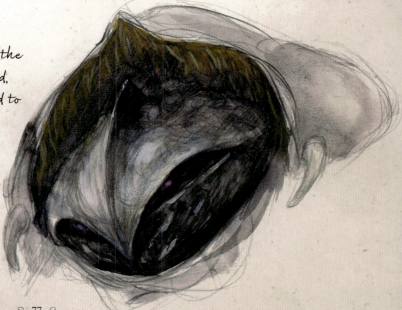

FIZZGIG

Fierce and furry, a Fizzgig's bark is rarely worse than its bite.
But its bark can still damage one's hearing.

    Fizzgigs are quadrupeds, standing on four small paws that
are usually concealed by the fur of their downy underbelly (or
"underfluff"). These paws are only used for short distance conveyance
though—Fizzgigs prefer to curl into a ball and roll to their
destination. To protect them during all this rolling, Fizzgigs have an
especially hard skull and a thick, shock-absorbent coat of fur.

Although Fizzgigs appear cute and fluffy, their bite radius is one of the largest on Thra, certainly in proportion to their diminutive size. Not only is their outer set of teeth impressive, but each Fizzgig has a second row of razor-sharp teeth circling their uvula. Naturally pack animals, a group of angry Fizzgigs can work together to fell prey many times their own size.

Fizzgigs make great companions and are regularly seen accompanying Gelfling and Podlings. Please note, however, they are fiercely independent and resent being labeled as pets. You have been warned.

LANDSTRIDER

Standing four or five times the height of a full-grown Gelfling, a galloping Landstrider is a visually imposing sight. But looks can be deceiving—Landstriders are peaceful, empathic animals that can be trained to become trusty steeds. Gelfling see the Landstrider-rider relationship as a partnership to be nurtured, rather than viewing the creatures simply as a form of conveyance.

Landstriders are resilient creatures with tough leathery hides and downy shocks of fur that they shed seasonally. Below their tangle of whiskers, Landstriders have small, toothless mouths with long, insectile tongues suited for lapping up nectar and stripping leaves from tall branches.

A Landstrider's stilt-like legs may appear fragile, but their fortified bones and joints are immensely durable. This ruggedness allows Landstriders to thrive in a number of habitats, including regions where their species does not naturally occur.

While mostly docile in nature, Landstriders are more than capable of defending themselves—and their riders—with powerful kicks.

FIRELING

The Fireling developed during the Age of Division and, as a result, are Thra's newest native species. They live in Mithra, under Thra's internal sun, thriving in the immense heat of the planet's core.

Fireling are direct descendants of Gelfling exiles and, apart from the wreath of magical flames that surrounds them, they physically resemble their forebears. Unlike their ancestors, however, Fireling cannot survive unaided in the cold and damp conditions found on Thra's surface—exposure to water can snuff out a Fireling's flame, instantly killing it.

Instead of dreamfasting, the Fireling firefast, communing with flames to see past events or emotions. A Gelfling and a Fireling can dreamfast together, but the results can be extremely painful for the Gelfling.

Though their own history is rife with tragedy and conflict, the Fireling remained ignorant of the horrors suffered by their Gelfling cousins in the world above. As a result, they reached the beginning of the Age of Power without any knowledge of the Skeksis and the blight they brought upon Thra.

PLUFF'M

Spirited and fuzzy, the diminutive Pluff'm have an inherent charm that has led many Gelfling to adopt them as pets—only to later discover the little creatures' intensely mischievous nature and an insatiable appetite for paper that has ruined many a family library.

Pluff'm stand as tall as a Podling's knee and are native to the Endless Forest, comfortable both on the forest floor and climbing the highest branches of the canopy.

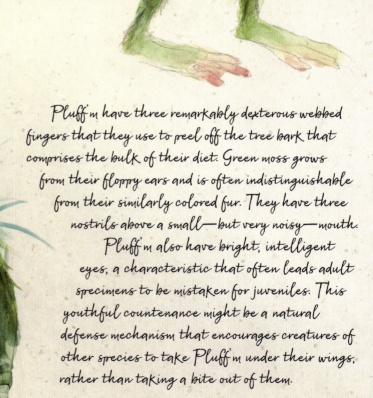

Pluff'm have three remarkably dexterous webbed fingers that they use to peel off the tree bark that comprises the bulk of their diet. Green moss grows from their floppy ears and is often indistinguishable from their similarly colored fur. They have three nostrils above a small—but very noisy—mouth. Pluff'm also have bright, intelligent eyes, a characteristic that often leads adult specimens to be mistaken for juveniles. This youthful countenance might be a natural defense mechanism that encourages creatures of other species to take Pluff'm under their wings, rather than taking a bite out of them.

ARMALIG

Stalwart beasts of burden, Armaligs are unmatched in both
power and speed. During the Age of Division, Skeksis
utilized trios of Armaligs to draw their royal carriages, the
creatures working together to pull the large, luxurious
coaches over long distances without needing to rest.

Armaligs are greenish in tint, with a domed head, segmented
insectile body, and large, sad eyes. Their six small, stocky
legs give them a distinctive trot that is neither imposing
nor graceful. But when their chitinous body segments are
tucked into a sphere, head under hind, these creatures can roll
themselves at incredible speed, attaining a momentum that can
knock down trees and crash through stone.

Wild Armaligs are mostly docile and indifferent to observers.
However, should a wild Armalig feel threatened, it will roll
away from danger at remarkable speed. And beware any
poor creature not fast enough to get out of its way!

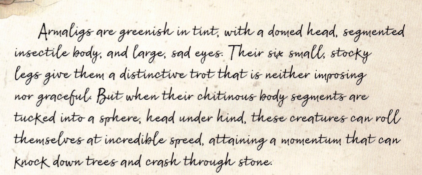

NURLOC

Large, peaceful, worm-like creatures, Nurlocs have long, ridged bodies that are specially adapted for crawling in and out of the caverns of Grot.

Adult Nurlocs have at least six eyes and continue to develop more as the segments of their bodies grow.

Nurlocs are farmed by the Grottan—Nurloc milk and cheese form the clan's main food source. When the creatures die, Grottan try to utilize every part of the Nurloc to honor the animals' lives. Nurloc leather is particularly valuable and prized for its softness.

Nurloc often give off a faint bioluminescent glow, the result of eating glow moss found within the Caves of Grot. Grottan shepherds know that a Nurloc that does not glow is likely to be in the early stages of malnourishment and should be moved to a new grazing ground.

Though they are generally peaceful, Nurlocs were
one of the first creatures on Thra to be exposed to the
Darkening, its effects making them violent, unpredictable,
and highly dangerous. Attempting to escape the caves,
many of these frenzied Nurlocs dug upward, concussing
themselves on layers of sediment before breaking through
to the surface and dying on the peaks of Grot, unable to
survive at such a high altitude.

NEBRIE

A fleshy, amphibious species, Nebrie have squat, grub-like bodies covered in a fine sheen of musky mucus that wards off potential predators. They are native to both Sog and to the wetlands of the Endless Forest and can often be found wallowing in nests of mud.

Nebrie have wide mouths—upturned in the corners to form what appears to be a friendly smile— and large ruby red eyes that sometimes glow when the creature is happy or excited.

Nebrie have a relatively short natural life span, which makes them the perfect livestock for Podlings, who eat only creatures that have died of natural causes. Female Nebrie are capable of producing many offspring over the trine or two they spend on Thra. Prized for their tasty and nutritious milk, the Nebrie is a highly valued creature within Podling society.

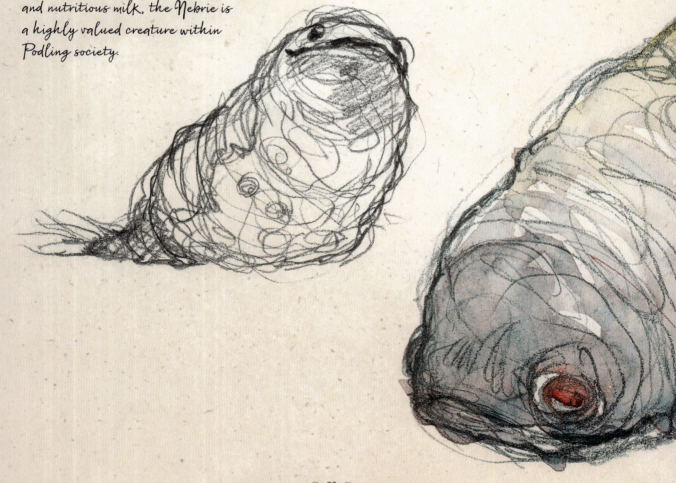

HOLLERBAT

Native to the Caves of Grot, Hollerbats have beady yellow eyes, a coat of rich dark red fur, and long arms that stretch into four sharp fingers. The fleshy membrane between these fingers allows Hollerbats to flit between stalactites and stalagmites—although they have a hard time flying great distances without frequently landing to rest.

Hollerbats have poor eyesight but—unlike many creatures of Grot—they do not ingest glow moss, so can't rely on its effects to light their way. Instead, they've developed the ability to "see" in the darkness by emitting a hollering cry that, when echoed back by objects in their surroundings, allows them to navigate with great dexterity.

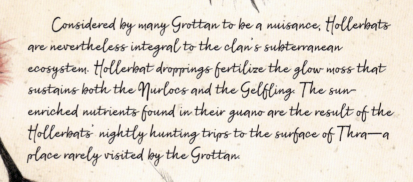

Considered by many Grottan to be a nuisance, Hollerbats are nevertheless integral to the clan's subterranean ecosystem. Hollerbat droppings fertilize the glow moss that sustains both the Nurlocs and the Gelfling. The sun-enriched nutrients found in their guano are the result of the Hollerbats' nightly hunting trips to the surface of Thra—a place rarely visited by the Grottan.

MOUNDER

Furry, horned farm animals that move in herds, Mounders can be shorn for their coarse wool or used to pull plows. Under their horns, Mounders have shriveled, wizened faces and lidded eyes. They use their large, multi-jointed hands to construct mounds of grass clods and soil that act as windbreaks against the elements. They are also able to construct rudimentary shelters. Farmers frequently leverage the Mounders' digging abilities to create irrigation channels.

Mounders are born with two "birth seeds" on their flanks. As they age, these seeds develop into saplings that keep growing until the Mounder reaches maturity. Dying when the Mounder is fully grown, the birth seeds leave behind two tree trunks embedded in the Mounder's flesh.

Although docile and slow-moving, Mounders are also intelligent and loyal. Herds of Mounders have been known to fight to protect their owner's land, and their presence is enough to dissuade most predators.

CRYSTAL SKIMMER

Enormous winged creatures with cartilaginous bodies and flat heads, Crystal Skimmers are perfectly adapted for life in the harsh, hot, arid climate of the Crystal Desert.

Although they have the largest wingspan of any creature on Thra, the featherless Crystal Skimmers do not often flap their wings, instead using them to effortlessly glide from place to place. They also hover by blasting heated air under their wings using their two long tail-like snouts.

Crystal Skimmers are constant companions of the Dousan and an important part of their culture and survival. Along with providing the Dousan with the means to navigate the treacherous wastes of the Crystal Desert, Crystal Skimmers can detect and warn of deadly sandstorms long before a Gelfling is able to see dust clouds on the horizon.

It takes many trine of training before a young Dousan is ready to pilot a Skimmer. Prospective captains must not only master the various hooks and stirrups used to guide the massive creature, they must also form a strong bond of trust with their Skimmer. Though it takes a team of crewmen to fly a Skimmer, Dousan captains are revered within the tribe, their skills enabling the fast transport of Gelfling and supplies, and quick getaways in the event of approaching sandstorms.

SIDETIC

A small flightless bird found scurrying across the floor of the Endless Forest, the Sidetic is notable for possessing beady eyes that move independently on short, crustacean-like stalks. The Sidetic has no wings at all, and its small, withered arms do not seem to serve any function. Fortunately, its beak is very strong and can be used to easily break open seedpods and nutshells. In the wild, the plumage of a Sidetic can flourish into a variety of colors, but when raised in captivity, the thin, fur-like feathers never develop beyond their original green. The Sidetic makes a charming pet—even skekTek the Scientist kept one as a companion. It was the only true friend the Skeksis ever had and although he spared it from his experiments, the atrocities the poor creature had to witness are best left unspoken.

SCRUMMUNCHER

Scrummunchers crave dead flesh. In the wild, these glossy beetle-like creatures can be found throughout Thra, wherever there is rot. Scrummunchers are scavengers, their hungry suction-cup mouths able to reduce a corpse to bare bones in mere hours. Although that may sound morbid, scrummunchers actually serve an important purpose. Their copious droppings return nutrients to Thra's soil much faster than regular decomposition.

In the Castle of the Crystal, scrummunchers are used during grooming rituals to chew calcified dead flesh from the Skeksis' feet and other extremities. For reasons inexplicable to science, they seem to find the waxen buildup between Skeksis' toes to be particularly delicious.

LOCKSNAKE

Found burrowing into the mountains of Grot and the cliffs of the Sifan Coast, the Locksnake is one of Thra's toughest creatures, its glistening hide nearly indestructible.

Locksnake babies are born pink and soft, but the moment they're free of their shells they begin to search for small pebbles and stones to ingest. Their digestive systems break down the rocks, allowing the juvenile Locksnakes to absorb mineral deposits directly into their flesh, their scales growing hard and metallic.

Full-grown Locksnakes move from eating stones to living prey, though they do still ingest rocks to maintain the toughness of their hides. Locksnakes range in color, their hue depending on the type of mineral deposits found in their diet.

Locksnakes have a unique skull structure that allows them to latch onto their own tail, forming an unbreakable loop. In the wild, they use this ability to trap and asphyxiate prey. Recognizing the creature's potential, the Skeksis use the Locksnake to secure their prized possessions. When placed around the handles of a door, cabinet, or chest, it can slither into place and join its head to its tail, creating an almost unbreakable bond. And if a would-be thief somehow manages to pry open a Locksnake, they are likely to find themselves on the receiving end of a deadly bite.

PEEPER BEETLE

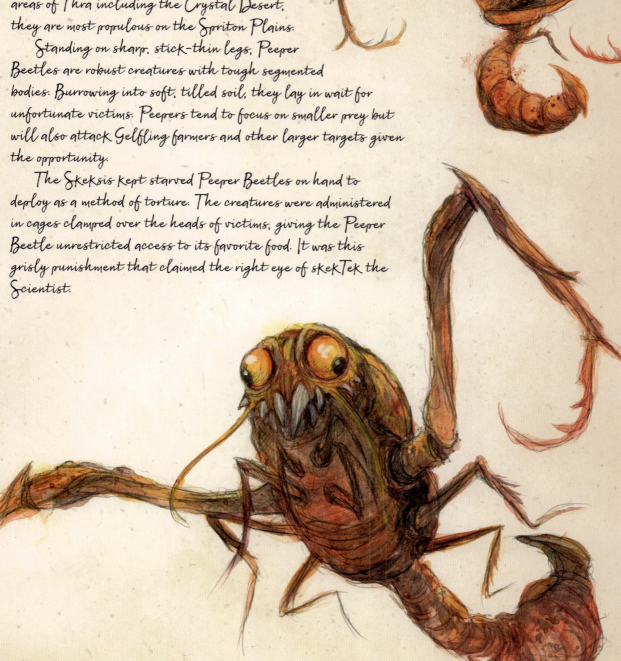

The fiendish Peeper Beetles crave the soft jelly found in fresh eyeballs and will attack any prey, big or small, to get it. Found in many areas of Thra including the Crystal Desert, they are most populous on the Spriton Plains.

Standing on sharp, stick-thin legs, Peeper Beetles are robust creatures with tough segmented bodies. Burrowing into soft, tilled soil, they lay in wait for unfortunate victims. Peepers tend to focus on smaller prey but will also attack Gelfling farmers and other larger targets given the opportunity.

The Skeksis kept starved Peeper Beetles on hand to deploy as a method of torture. The creatures were administered in cages clamped over the heads of victims, giving the Peeper Beetle unrestricted access to its favorite food. It was this grisly punishment that claimed the right eye of skekTek the Scientist.

THRUSHPOG

No creature better exemplifies the connection between all life on Thra than the humble Thrushpog. Both plant and animal, individual being and interconnected nest, Thrushpogs grow from the knots and burls of trees in the Endless Forest. A Thrushpog has a slender neck that terminates in a round stomach chamber. It also has two petals at the top of its stem that pick up vibrations, just like ears. At the base of the Thrushpog sits a bowl-shaped shell that anchors the creature to a host tree. In this symbiotic relationship, Thrushpogs share their nutrients and collected rainwater with the tree in exchange for shelter and safety.

Thrushpogs inhabit trees in groups, each member connected by thin, fibrous tubers that run within and over the tree's bark and flesh. These families are also linked to further Thrushpog communities situated in neighboring trees via the root system of their host.

A network of Thrushpogs can stretch from the heart of Sami Thicket all the way past the borders of the Stonewood Clan. They are a reminder that all are one, regardless of the tribal boundaries and other distractions that sometimes cloud the true nature of Thra.

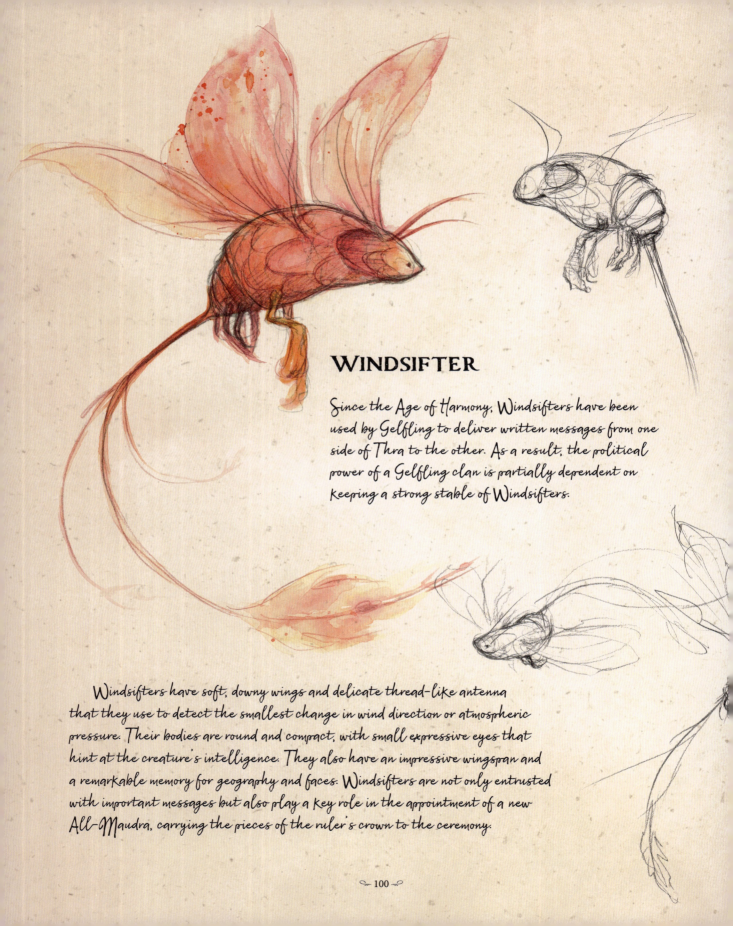

WINDSIFTER

Since the Age of Harmony, Windsifters have been used by Gelfling to deliver written messages from one side of Thra to the other. As a result, the political power of a Gelfling clan is partially dependent on keeping a strong stable of Windsifters.

Windsifters have soft, downy wings and delicate thread-like antenna that they use to detect the smallest change in wind direction or atmospheric pressure. Their bodies are round and compact, with small expressive eyes that hint at the creature's intelligence. They also have an impressive wingspan and a remarkable memory for geography and faces. Windsifters are not only entrusted with important messages but also play a key role in the appointment of a new All-Maudra, carrying the pieces of the ruler's crown to the ceremony.

There are many different varieties, from the
majestically decorated Great Scarlet Windsifter
to the unremarkably adorned Lowlands
Speckled Windsifter. Many Gelfling have
dedicated their lives to the training and
preservation of Windsifters, even introducing
new varieties through selective breeding.

UNAMOTH

Naturally occurring in all but the most inhospitable regions of Thra, Unamoths begin life as tiny larvae, no bigger than a Podling thumb. Once they gestate and unfurl their massive, segmented wings, however, they can grow several times larger than some varieties of predatory birds.

The chrysalis that
a larval Unamoth builds
as part of its transition to
adulthood is an intricate and
colorful creation reminiscent of
blown glass. The Vapra, who've taken
the adult Unamoth as their clan sigil,
prize these pupae for their beautiful
aesthetic properties, while Sifan
soothsayers believe them to be
sacred objects that represent
the ever-changing
stages of life.

MOOG

One of the few burrowing mammals that can survive in the Crystal Desert, the Moog is often found with only its eyes and nose protruding from behind its heavily armored body plates, its tail and hind legs buried beneath the sand.

The Moog has ridged, conical arms that it uses to dig deep below the sand in search of precious cooling moisture. Moogs have even been known to dig so deep that they reveal underground springs, inadvertently bringing water to the surface and creating small oases.

While the Dousan use Moog bones for adornment and rituals, they consider it bad luck to kill the creatures. Not only can a Moog help scent water, but the creatures are rapacious insectivores that keep the Crystal Sea's population of stinging and biting insects in check, a proclivity greatly appreciated by the Dousan.

CRYSTAL BAT

Like the Garthim, Crystal Bats are another Skeksis-engineered species. Both animal and mineral, the winged beasts were fitted with a hexagonal crystal at their center that allowed them to broadcast everything they observed back to the Castle of the Crystal.

Invented by the Skeksis during the Garthim War, the Crystal Bats were dispatched into the skies of Thra in such numbers that clouds of the winged spies blotted out the suns. Their numbers were so great that the Skeksis lost track of entire schools of the creatures. Free of their cruel masters, these unsupervised roosts of Crystal Bats lived their lives peacefully into the Age of Power, even picking up behavioral traits from their organic cousins, the Hollerbats.

PHILLIITE

If a stone formation appears to have massive eyebrows, lips, and a nose, it may well be a dozing Philliite. These enormous talking rocks are immobile creatures who, unable to hunt or graze, receive nearly all their nourishment from the lichens and mosses that grow on the inside of their mouths. (They've also been known to consume any animals foolish enough to wander onto their stone tongues, squeezing them of nutrients in a digestion process that can last for a full season.)

Although they will speak to anyone who will listen, their language is unintelligible, and regional variations of their dialect further impede any attempts at translation. Only Mother Aughra has ever successfully held a conversation with a Philliite. Sadly, she found the creature to be an overwhelming bore.

FIREBUG

Small, balloon-shaped insects, Firebugs give off a warm amber glow. At birth, a young Firebug's body inflates with natural luminous gasses, rising into the air and not touching the ground until death.

Firebugs are used by the Stonewood Clan as a means of illumination. Placed in large mesh pens where Gelfling lamplighters keep the creatures well fed with the nectar that fuels their luminescence, Firebugs are quite content in captivity.

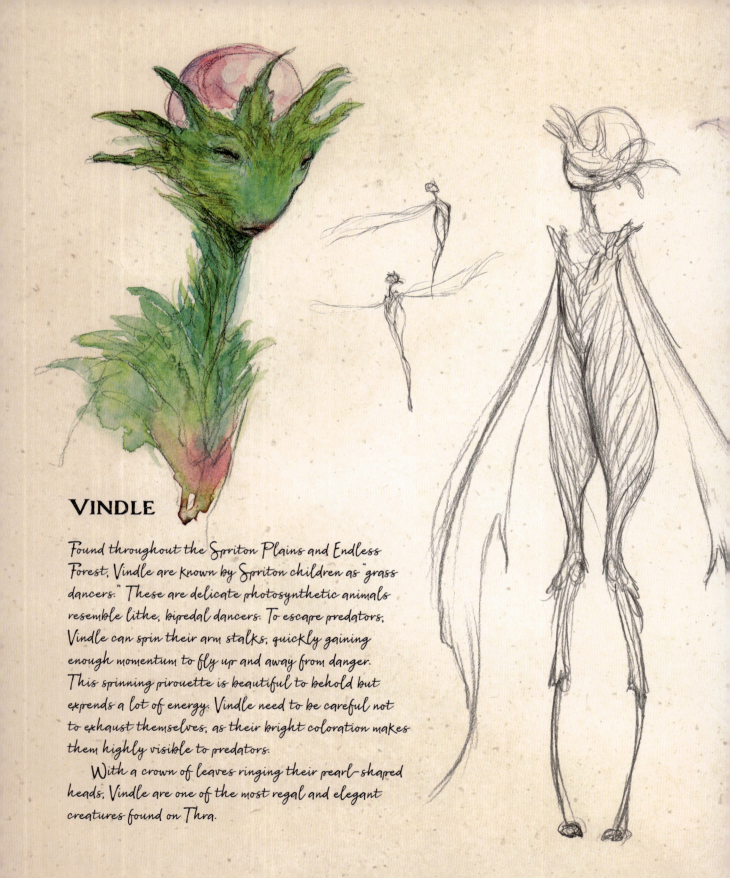

VINDLE

Found throughout the Spriton Plains and Endless
Forest, Vindle are known by Spriton children as "grass
dancers." These are delicate photosynthetic animals
resemble lithe, bipedal dancers. To escape predators,
Vindle can spin their arm stalks, quickly gaining
enough momentum to fly up and away from danger.
This spinning pirouette is beautiful to behold but
expends a lot of energy. Vindle need to be careful not
to exhaust themselves, as their bright coloration makes
them highly visible to predators.

    With a crown of leaves ringing their pearl-shaped
heads, Vindle are one of the most regal and elegant
creatures found on Thra.

BOHRTOG

A luminous flying eel, the Bohrtog is not a creature of Thra but was instead transported to the planet from the urSkek home world during the Age of Power. The Bohrtog was large enough to carry several Gelfling on its back, its magical speed and strength an asset to Jen and Kira during their reign over the Gelfling nation.

AWLIS

Large birds capable of lifting a full-grown Podling off the ground, Awlis are formidable hunters. With dark purple satin plumage and large, bright reflective eyes, they are beautiful, haunting creatures.

    The Awlis has an enormous wingspan and can cover a hundred wheels of hunting ground in a night. It can also turn its head in full rotation by detaching its neck bone from its skull, ensuring no prey can escape the scope of its vision.

    Proportionately, baby Awlis have even larger eyes than their parents and a series of thin feathers that stick straight up like antennae. Endearingly adorable, baby Awlis that fall from their nests are sometimes adopted by Gelfling, often unaware of how big—and fearsome—the creatures will one day become.

As twilight falls over the Endless Forest,
the Awlis bays the night song of Thra's
woodlands. For smaller creatures scampering
across the forest floor, the cry is a death
knell. Many Gelfling poets have tried
to replicate the Awlis' song in words and
dreametchings, but all have failed.

BOVART

Found in the mountains outside Ha'rar and at the base of the Endless Forest, the Bovart is a fuzzy, four-eyed creature notable for the patches of bright ginger fur that cover stretches of its pale tan flesh. The Bovart has no natural camouflage against its environment, but then again, it doesn't need it.

A Bovart's four sinewy legs are spring-loaded at the knee, and its four powerful eyes allow it to hunt its prey from a great distance. When it spies prey, the Bovart launches itself into a giant leap, and with its broad, callused feet, it squashes the unsuspecting quarry flat before making a meal out of the resulting mess.

Because of the rotten guts that amass between their toes over time, Bovart smell quite terrible.

BUBLUP

With squat, spherical bodies set on thin, lanky legs, a Bublup is undeniably comical in appearance. Its normal bipedal gate is gangly and awkward, and when threatened, a Bublup will attempt to escape predators by performing a series of evasive cartwheels.

Bublup have multiple mouths, some so small they're barely visible. They feed by burying themselves in soil and using their filter-like mouths to sift tiny bugs and nutrients from the soil. Found in the Spriton Plains and the surrounding woods, they are often confused for root vegetables by Podling foragers. Sometimes this case of mistaken identity can be deadly for the Bublup. It's not an easy life.

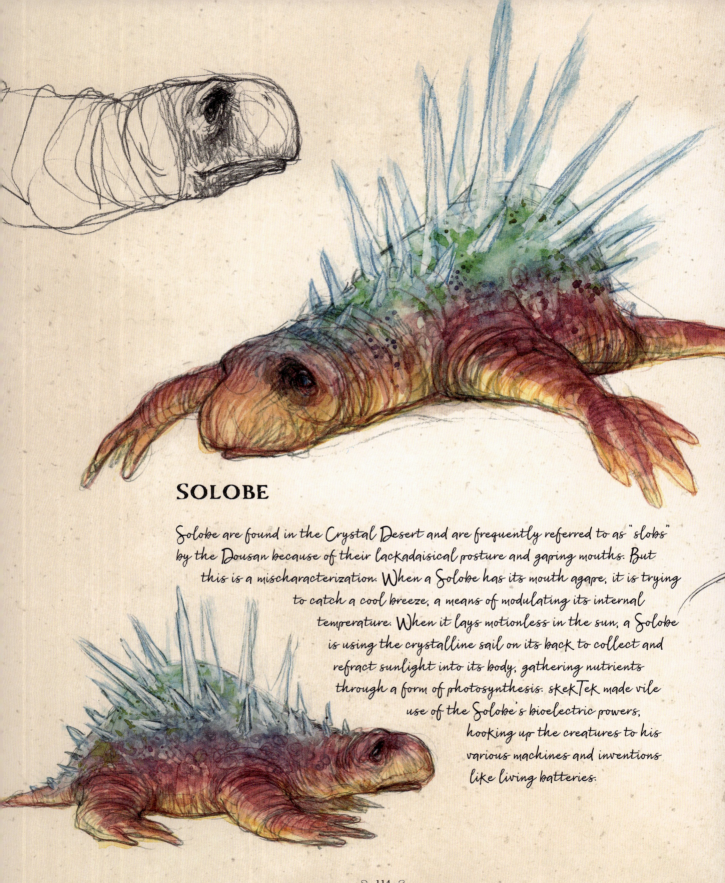

SOLOBE

Solobe are found in the Crystal Desert and are frequently referred to as "slobs" by the Dousan because of their lackadaisical posture and gaping mouths. But this is a mischaracterization. When a Solobe has its mouth agape, it is trying to catch a cool breeze, a means of modulating its internal temperature. When it lays motionless in the sun, a Solobe is using the crystalline sail on its back to collect and refract sunlight into its body, gathering nutrients through a form of photosynthesis. skekTek made vile use of the Solobe's bioelectric powers, hooking up the creatures to his various machines and inventions like living batteries.

HOWEFROC

Natives of the grasslands outside the Valley of the Mystics and of sparser sections of the Endless Forest, Howefroc are covered in long, soft fur that grows over the patches of bony armor covering their bodies.

Howefroc use their long, curved claws for climbing, their armor and fur forming an effective protective padding that saves them from injury in the event of a fall.

As Howefroc age, their armored plates grow, eventually becoming so unwieldy that they begin to restrict the creatures' movement. Fortunately, Howefroc are social creatures that have learned to use rocks and other tools to groom their compatriots, filing down the obstructive plates as needed.

Teberfroc

Teberfroc have brown, brindled fur, marble eyes, and two thin antennae. Their delicate padded paws are used to dig up the tubers and roots that make up the majority of their diet. These uncommonly fastidious creatures tend to live near ponds and streams in the Endless Forest, not only to drink but to wash their paws clean.

Teberfroc sleep for the majority of the day, often choosing shallow burrows and fallen logs as resting spots—locations that do not offer adequate sanctuary. Due to their incautious nature, they are frequently caught unawares by predators.

The Teberfroc has escaped extinction largely due to Gelfling compassion—Stonewood and Spriton foresters frequently pick up vulnerable, dozing Teberfroc and move them to safer resting spots.

GOBBLES

Gobbles are tiny, spherical bulbs that grow on the forest floor in clusters of thousands. At first glance they may seem harmless, but nothing could be further from the truth. These opportunistic predators each have an oversize mouth ringed with rows of sharp, needle-like teeth. Each row is able to rotate independently, the spiral motion creating a buzz-saw effect that rends and mulches flesh and bone in seconds.

A colony of Gobbles can survive on a relatively small amount of prey, a necessary capability for a creature that is permanently anchored in place, gaining sustenance solely from the misadventure of other animals. Upon feeding, a mass of Gobbles is able to redistribute nutrients to other less well-fed Gobbles patches via a stem network, demonstrating that there is more to these creatures than their rapacious appetites.

IPSY

An Ipsy is a large, dark green insect that walks on its hind legs. Found in the Endless Forest, Ipsy are generally peaceful, gentle creatures—that is until mating season arrives.

Before the female Ipsy chooses a husband, two males must fight for her affections. These contests of strength and bravado are more ceremonial than combative, and the loser is often left unscathed. That's more than can be said for the winner, who after mating is pulled limb from limb by the female Ipsy.

Stonewood children often collect large groups of Ipsy and use the creatures to stage gladiatorial battles. Once a victor has been named, the children safely return the honorable champion and competitors to the wild.

DRUMLUR

Drumlur stay hydrated by soaking their root-like feet in the marshlands of Sog. This practice often leads these unique creatures to be mistaken for plants. A single Drumlur is no heavier than a blade of grass, but by combining forces they are able to form a sturdy mass and assist one another in feeding on swamp slop. A large gathering of Drumlur is known as a stack.

When a stack needs to find a fresher body of water, Drumlur simply pick up their feet and walk as one, moving the entire stack to a new location with a squeaky rustling sound. Such migrations can be so disruptive to the geography of the marshlands that Drenchen sometimes find themselves lost in their own swamps.

GIZZIZZY

Found in both Sog and the Endless Forest, the Gizzizzy is a brown and orange amphibian with four stubby feet and a long tail. Because Gizzizzy are frequent preyed upon by larger animals, females of the species have evolved to lay multiple clutches of eggs per trine, ensuring their population remains robust. As part of the birthing process, the mothers push their small translucent eggs through their skin. Once hatched, the offspring cling to the backs of both parents—sometimes dozens at a time—until they feel brave enough to drop off and venture out into the world on their own.

Sharp Awlid

The diurnal cousin of the Awlis, Sharp Awlids look similar to their relatives but have much brighter plumage that incorporates vibrant blues and yellows. Their song is also more flamboyant and delivered in a higher tonal range that is sweeter to the ear.

Sharp Awlids nest in the mountaintops outside Ha'rar and are able to fly at such incredible altitudes that when they dive back to the ground their talons and feathers are often tipped with frost.

As they grow, Sharp Awlids shed and regrow their beaks, the new bills coming through with a fresh golden sheen and a sharp edge. Vapra treasure hunters have been known to bring these beaks back from the mountains believing they have struck gold, only to have their hopes dashed by local merchants.

SONTONIC

Sontonic are small mammals that prefer to live near brackish water. They have compact facial features, wriggling noses, and hundreds of sharp quills lining their backs. In the wild, a Sontonic's mossy quills trap seeds, spores, and other flora until the little creature begins to resemble a traveling garden. Sadly, this colorful display makes them easy targets for predators. It's fortunate then that Sontonic also flourish in captivity—the Drenchen and Stonewood keep them as pets, often utilizing the spiny critters as living scrub brushes.

GUFFLE

Guffle are known for being hedonistic eaters with a propensity for breaking wind at ear-splitting volume. Apart from their poor table manners, they are extremely agreeable creatures with highly distinctive features, including shiny black eyes and chubby whisker-rimmed snouts.

Although warm-blooded, Guffle are equally at home on land or in water. Expert swimmers, they are unperturbed by harsh waters and are protected from freezing temperatures by a layer of insulating blubber. In their never-ending hunt for fish and land-based prey, Guffle have been known to find their way from the swamps and estuaries of Sog all the way out to the Silver Sea.

The Skeksis kept Guffle under their banquet tables to clean up food scraps—the subsequent emissions released by the little creatures were sometimes loud enough to make even the Gourmand blush. Unsurprisingly, the Skeksis would frequently blame their own gaseous output on the creatures. Sadly, after these captive Guffle had been properly fattened up over a trine or two, they would end up on the table, rather than under it.

KARATICK

Denizens of the Crystal Desert, Karaticks are notable for the dark, fluffy feathers that cover sections of their body while leaving portions of their legs and underside exposed. During the day, when the suns are at their highest, the Karatick can shift its body so that its feathers protect its naked flesh from sunburn. Similarly, when night comes and the temperature drops, the Karatick covers these exposed sections with down, fluffing its feathers into a configuration that better holds in heat.

Karatick are naturally insectivores, but when violent sandstorms decimate their feeding grounds, they have been known to become carnivorous, even turning to cannibalism.

PIMLIN

With its fine coat of thick
green fur accentuated by long pale feathers,
the Pimlin shares many aesthetic similarities
with the Sidetic, although it is actually a
mammal rather than a bird. A creature of Sog,
the Pimlin builds its nests using swamp mosses
and feeds itself on marshland tree leaves and insects.
One of the most elusive of Thra's species, the last known
captive Pimlin was dissected in skekTek's lab late in the Age of
Division. skekTek's only note about the specimen was that the
color of its blood "matched its fur, a pleasant green hue."

BRIGHT SCHEZZ

As the Bright Schezz waddles along the Endless Forest floor, it waves its three-pronged, feathered proboscis like a dowsing rod. Able to sense minute changes in air quality, it sifts through thousands of scents, locating small prey with pinpoint accuracy. When the Bright Schezz scents a nearby treat, its thin, furry toes spread wide and it transitions from an awkward waddle to a headlong sprint. In hunting mode, a Bright Schezz moves as a purple blur, its prey blissfully unaware until it's in the Schezz's stomach.

RIDDIT

Riddit have bulbous eyes and a shock of fur running down their backs. Making their home beneath the Endless Forest's topsoil, Riddit communicate using a bubble-like vocal sac to emit the "riddit, riddit, riddit" croaking sound from which their name is derived.

The Riddit uses its clawed forepaws to burrow elaborate tunnels that weave in and out of the root systems of large trees. These underground tunnel networks become vast Riddit societies complete with breeding chambers. Often the tunnels are so numerous that they cause trees above to topple, disrupting the surface world and setting off minor underground cave-ins.

GRIDIT

The aboveground cousin of the Riddit, Gridit are solitary creatures that make their homes near streams in the Endless Forest or in Sog's copses of tall grass.

Gridit have rubbery skin and pliable, cartilaginous bones. Their most notable feature is the row of suction cups that runs down their four legs and allows them to grip the smooth rocks of the riverbeds where they hunt. Gridit thrive on moisture and can often be found dozing in puddles after rainfall, their pores soaking up the muddy water.

If there's a drought, a Gridit will expel all the water from its body and enter a state of suspended animation until the rains return, rejuvenating the desiccated creature.

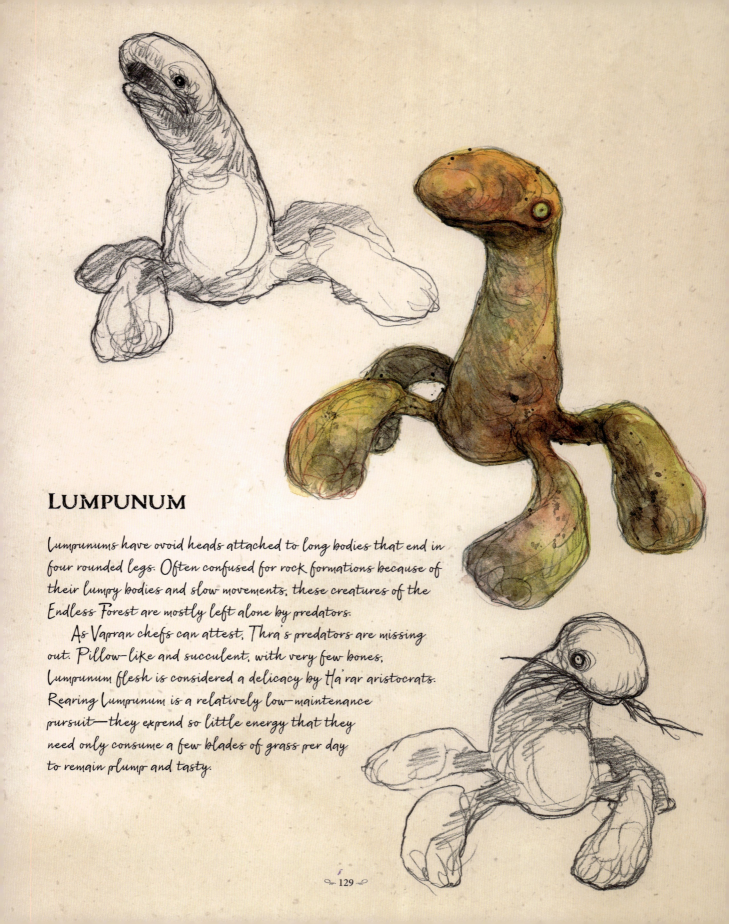

LUMPUNUM

Lumpunums have ovoid heads attached to long bodies that end in four rounded legs. Often confused for rock formations because of their lumpy bodies and slow movements, these creatures of the Endless Forest are mostly left alone by predators.

As Vapran chefs can attest, Thra's predators are missing out. Pillow-like and succulent, with very few bones, Lumpunum flesh is considered a delicacy by Ha'rar aristocrats. Rearing Lumpunum is a relatively low-maintenance pursuit—they expend so little energy that they need only consume a few blades of grass per day to remain plump and tasty.

FLINGIT

One of Sog's most common creatures, Flingits are often sighted as a clump of wet hair, floating along the surface of the marshes. But underneath that thick, luxurious mop is a wide-mouthed amphibian, ready to lap up passing insects with its sticky tongue.

Drenchen avoid Flingits because of the mistaken belief that they spread warts; in fact, the creature's mucus possesses acute medicinal qualities. Sifan sailors, on the other hand, are well aware of Flingit healing properties and keep the creatures onboard their ships—sick sailors need only lick the belly of a Flingit to begin feeling its potent healing effects.

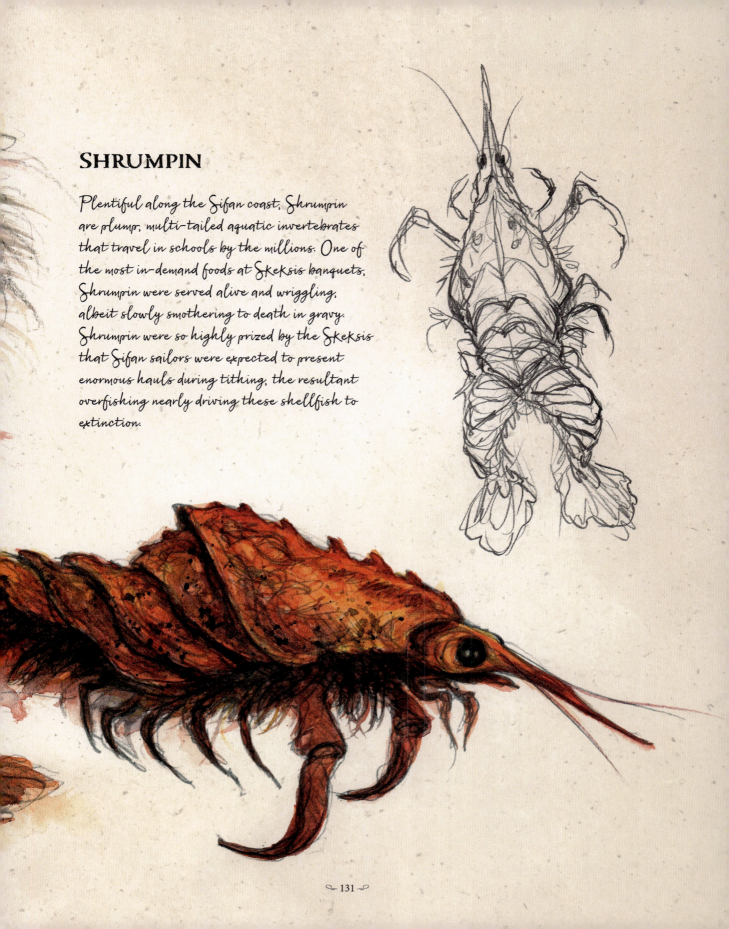

SHRUMPIN

Plentiful along the Sifan coast, Shrumpin are plump, multi-tailed aquatic invertebrates that travel in schools by the millions. One of the most in-demand foods at Skeksis banquets, Shrumpin were served alive and wriggling, albeit slowly smothering to death in gravy. Shrumpin were so highly prized by the Skeksis that Sifan sailors were expected to present enormous hauls during tithing, the resultant overfishing nearly driving these shellfish to extinction.

TORTLE

Massive shelled reptiles whose physiology incorporates flesh, scales, and stone, adult Tortles can hibernate for many trine, slowing down their metabolism to the point where they appear to be deceased. Tortles often awaken from their slumber to find entire ecosystems living on their backs, including trees, birds, and animals.

Often sighted swimming in the Silver Sea, Tortles are able to hibernate while afloat, inevitably becoming floating islands that sustain pockets of life as they drift around Thra's shores.

Born out of eggs the size of Podlings, Tortle infants were another Skeksis delicacy. The unfortunate newborns were served live inside pies—the crust a mix of flour and the Tortle's own amniotic fluid. Often, the young Tortles ate their way out of the pie, only to be quickly gobbled up by gluttonous Skeksis.

LEFAR WORM

Dig into soil anywhere on Thra and, chances are, you'll find a writhing mass of Lefar Worms. Even during the blighted and desolate days late in the Age of Division, when the Dark Crystal was at its most volatile, Lefar Worms still managed to thrive. Lefar Worms remain one of the hardiest life-forms on Thra, capable of completely regenerating from any wound, no matter how grievous. They can even recover after being split in half, one Lefar Worm becoming two. They are also a good source of nutrition—the Skeksis were particularly fond of Lefar Worms, consuming them in wriggling handfuls.

HUMHED

If a Humhed, with its curved spiral shell and myriad sticky
tentacles, looks out of place in the Endless Forest, that's
because it is. Humheds are born at sea, and when fully grown,
they swim inland, following the river deltas and inlets in search
of prey. Humheds have large green eyes that allow them to see
at night or in deep, murky waters, and their angular heads and
long neck stalks are similar in texture to their scaled tentacles.
When threatened, the Humhed is able to collapse its entire body,
including its skull, into a floppy mass of tissue
easily retracted into its shell. Many of these
woodland mollusks never return to salt water and
live the entirety of their lives under the cover of
the forest's thick canopy.

LIFFIZER

Liffizers are creatures of the Endless Forest identifiable by their twitchy suspicious eyes and long, powerful legs.

Jumpy creatures, both literally and figuratively, Liffizers can perform an impressive vertical leap that allows them to reach the highest branches of berry bushes and legume trees. When they find a food source, they quickly strip it of as much nourishment as possible, while trying to avoid the attention of circling Awlises. They gobble up these nuts and berries but don't swallow, instead storing their finds in large cheek pouches.

Back at their nests, Liffizers regurgitate the day's harvest. Their saliva acts as a preservative, keeping the foraged food fresh for a whole season.

TWO-EYED STICKLER

When traveling to the Endless Forest, one might be tempted to pat the innocent-looking Two-Eyed Stickler's inviting, crystalline fur.

    Do not touch it!

A tiny bead of poison tips every hair on a Two-Eyed Stickler's body—on contact, the victim's muscles instantly lock up and become wracked with searing pain that can last hours. If exposed, Stonewood locals say the best cure is chugging Nebrie milk. If Nebrie milk is in short supply, one should lie still on the ground (preferably some distance from any other Two-Eyed Sticklers) and prepare to cry, scream, and wail for a full rotation of the Greater Sun.

    Though perilous to harvest, Two-Eyed Stickler poison has many uses—skekMal the Hunter would frequently tip his hunting snares with the substance, a wholly effective way to subdue prey.

DUBABUB

One of the most graceful swimmers in the Silver Sea,
an adult Dubabub can grow as many as eighteen fins, which it uses in
perfect synchronicity to paddle through the water. The Dubabub is a
social creature that is frequently sighted swimming in large groups, its
long neck gliding above the waterline. Able to band together to ward
off any potential threats, Dubabub have few natural predators. Pods of
Dubabub can be seen frolicking in the surf along the Sifan Coast, while
sightings further out at sea are considered auspicious
omens by Sifan sailors.

TENDRIL

Pink and gelatinous, Tendrils are found on the hills along the Sifan Coast, as well as in the Endless Forest and the mountain ranges approaching the Castle of the Crystal. Tendrils lie motionless for hours waiting for a bug or small mammal to crawl past before lashing out with their neurotoxic feelers. Even the faintest graze will paralyze small prey so that the Tendril can stuff the still-living morsel into its mouth.

Though mostly sedentary, whole colonies of Tendrils can roll to a new cliff face like tumbleweeds when food in their current location becomes scarce.

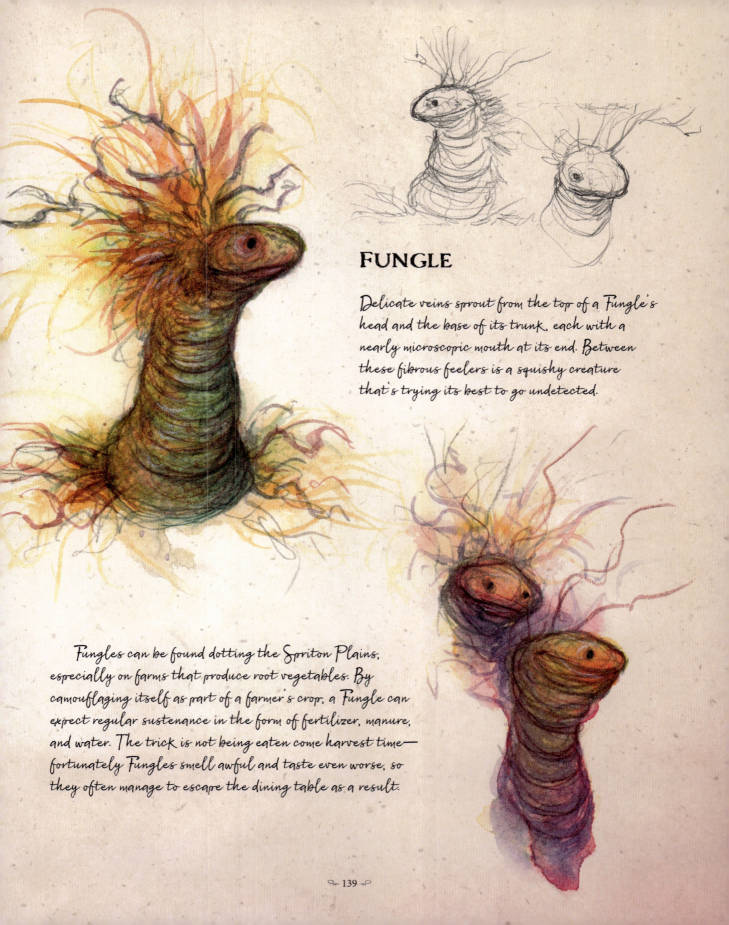

FUNGLE

Delicate veins sprout from the top of a Fungle's head and the base of its trunk, each with a nearly microscopic mouth at its end. Between these fibrous feelers is a squishy creature that's trying its best to go undetected.

Fungles can be found dotting the Spriton Plains, especially on farms that produce root vegetables. By camouflaging itself as part of a farmer's crop, a Fungle can expect regular sustenance in the form of fertilizer, manure, and water. The trick is not being eaten come harvest time—fortunately Fungles smell awful and taste even worse, so they often manage to escape the dining table as a result.

ARMORED BUB

Few creatures of Thra have a name more apt than the Armored Bub,
a mammal with a thick outer shell that bellows "Bub, bub, bub"
as it sniffs around the arid climes of the Crystal Desert. One of
the Peeper Beetle's few natural predators, the Armored Bub
resorts to eating desert scrub if it cannot find meatier
fare. Because Peeper Beetles present a serious threat to
desert travelers, the Armored Bub is revered in Dousan
culture for its role in keeping the eye-
munching insects at bay.

CRAWLIE

Crawlies are chirping fuzzballs with long, feathery feelers on either side, which they use to change direction when rolling toward their destination. Pests and scavengers, Crawlies are most often found in and around settlements. They took root at the Castle of the Crystal after several specimens escaped from a banquet where they were to be served as dessert. Soon breeding themselves into a full-grown infestation, the Crawlies were regularly hunted down by Podling servants, tasked with catching the fast-moving delicacy for their masters.

SQUIDDLEITCH

Squiddleitch are invertebrates found in the swamplands of Sog, identifiable by their six muscular tentacles and their fleshy bodies. Omnivorous, the Squiddleitch's diet mostly consists of fish, although it also constantly nibbles lichen and algae as it clings to stones or fallen logs. Fried Squiddleitch was a favorite main course at the Skeksis banquet table. As a result, the Drenchen hunted them to near extinction to pay Skeksis tithes during the Age of Division. Though Squiddleitch are not aggressive by nature, they will fiercely defend themselves when attacked, lashing out with their tentacles to deliver a blow that's strong enough to pop a Drenchen's shoulder right out of its socket.

CUPPATI

Essentially a mop of orange fur with protruding fangs and large black eyes, Cuppati can be found crawling along the ridges and overhangs of the Sifan Coast. They frequently raid unattended birds' nests, eating the eggs before blending into the natural camouflage of the nest. When the mother bird returns home, the main course of the Cuppati's meal begins.

Z'NID BIRD

Z'nid Birds are the natural predators of the Nurloc and are so tenacious and cunning that Grottan shepherds struggle to keep them from decimating their flocks.

Hunting in packs, Z'nid Birds have barbed tails that they use to inject their prey with a corrosive venom that not only kills their quarry but begins the work of digesting the corpse before the Z'nids have even begun eating. Once their prey has stopped twitching, Z'nid Birds descend on the prey in large groups and use their sucker-shaped mouths to slurp up the melted Nurloc flesh.

Due to the stealthy nature of the Z'nid Bird, few witness their attacks. It is not uncommon for Grottan shepherds to wake to find their entire herd of Nurlocs has been devoured in a single nighttime raid.

TIDLEBIT

Descendants of simple life-forms that existed at the birth of Thra, Tidlebit are puddle dwellers that crawl along the bottom of ancient tide pools in the deepest regions of Grot. Though their anatomy is simple, they have developed a rudimentary language, purring and bubbling away in the darkness, even pausing to let their neighbors in nearby pools speak. Their main source of sustenance is Hollerbat guano, which can be found in ample supply in the Caves of Grot.

BROWN SLIPPLY

This aquatic bird may not be aerodynamic, but what it lacks in airborne grace it makes up for in swimming ability. Spherical with a slender, hooked beak built for skewering Shrumpin, Brown Slipply spin their bodies in the water as they dive for their prey, leaving small whirlpools in their wake.

Brown Slipply make their nests high in the cliffs of the Sifan Coast. Not long after a newborn hatches, it must make the journey from the cliffs to the Silver Sea, the chick's parents ensuring that their offspring exits the nest at high tide to avoid being smashed against the rocks below.

FEATHERED PINCH

Feathered Pinches excel at making life difficult for the animals that inhabit the Endless Forest, attaching themselves to larger creatures' underbellies in order to hitch a ride to more fertile hunting grounds. Using their two front claws to clamp themselves in place, Feathered Pinches are extremely difficult to displace and only let go of their hosts when they sense nearby prey. A Feathered Pinch's favorite meal is Bublup, which they pick apart leg by leg before consuming the ball-like body.

ROUND BOB

Sharp balls of teeth with pointed quills, these deep-sea creatures range in color from brilliant amber to dark purple. Their razor-sharp teeth are irregularly shaped and have a lacquered sheen.

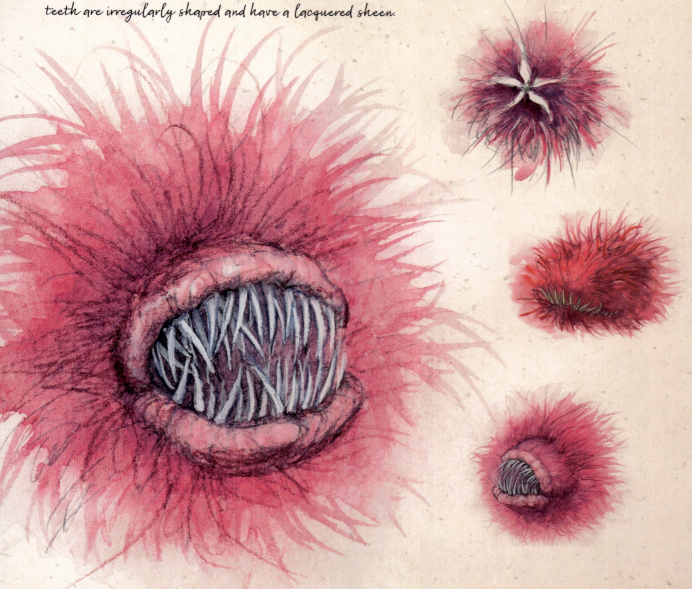

Found throughout the Silver Sea, these rapacious creatures are known by Sifan sailors as the Gobbles of the sea. Completely inedible, Round Bobs often get tangled in fishing nets and need to be carefully removed and tossed overboard before the rest of the catch can be harvested.

MULLIP

Mullips are one of
nature's great imitators.
Found on the southern coasts of Thra,
Mullips climb to the top of fruiting trees
before retracting into their circular, patterned
shells. There, the Mullip shifts the color of
its shell to become indistinguishable from the fruit that
surrounds it. When a hungry herbivore tries to take a bite out of
the Mullip, the camouflaged creature strikes, latching on with
its pointed, hollow claws and pumping its victim full of a venom
that liquefies flesh and internal organs. Once the poison has
done its hideous work, the Mullip drinks its prey, sucking up
the goop through its whisker-like proboscises.

THREE-EYED CRUDDER

Three-Eyed Crudder are fast-growing barnacle-like creatures found clinging to docks and the undersides of ships. Their bodies are composed of hundreds of fine bristles called baleen. The Three-Eyed Crudder spends its entire life waiting for the sea to provide its meals, the ebb and flow of the water bringing small plant and animal particulates into its baleen, then down to its stomach.

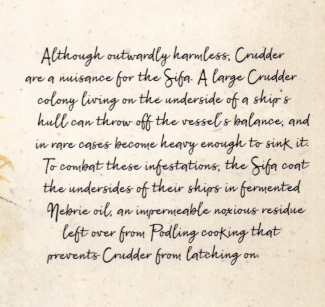

Although outwardly harmless, Crudder are a nuisance for the Sifa. A large Crudder colony living on the underside of a ship's hull can throw off the vessel's balance, and in rare cases become heavy enough to sink it. To combat these infestations, the Sifa coat the undersides of their ships in fermented Nebrie oil, an impermeable noxious residue left over from Podling cooking that prevents Crudder from latching on.

BRINDLISK

Massive horned beetles with crimson shells, Brindlisk make temporary homes in burrows deep in the sands of the Sifan coast. Feeding on small saltwater invertebrates caught up in tide pools, Brindlisk are nomadic, never staying on one stretch of beach for more than a few days.

Because of their vibrant coloration, Brindlisk are often the first thing Sifan sailors spot when returning to land. The similarly nomadic Sifa feel a great kinship with the Brindlisk, wearing jewelry made from their bright red shells for luck.

FRAGOR

The Fragor of Mithra are a multi-limbed race of sentient insects notable for their searing red carapaces. These fiery creatures frequently clashed with their neighbors, the Fireling, throughout the Age of Division and the Age of Power, their contentious relationship mirroring that of the Gelfling and the Arathim.

Dangerous as individuals, but truly frightening as a group, Fragor can vibrate the tendons on their abdomens to produce a deafeningly loud shrieking noise. When "harmonizing" these screams, Fragor create a cacophony so powerful it can demolish solid objects and liquefy Fireling soldiers.

SEEDLE

Seedles are massive, gentle creatures that hold within them the secret to the Endless Forest's expansion and regeneration. A juvenile Seedle has slitted glowing eyes, broad wooden teeth, and a young forest growing from its body.

When a Seedle reaches adulthood, it adopts a prone position, ceases all movement, and begins to grow roots. This marks the end of the Seedle's life cycle, but the creature is far from dead. From its body a mass of new forest growth sprouts. It is no longer a singular sentient creature but a wellspring of woodland life.

Populous in the Age of Harmony, Seedles became increasingly rare during the Age of Division, having been virtually wiped out by the spread of the Darkening. This scarcity slowed the expansion of the Endless Forest, which finally halted when there were no more Seedles to be found.

153

LUNARKIN

Delicate, air-filled creatures that float in the skies above the temperate zones of Thra, Lunarkin are often mistaken for dense cloud cover. Migratory creatures that can cover great distances at high altitudes, Lunarkin have been known to drift from the Spriton Plains to the Castle of the Crystal in less than a day. Intrepid Gelfling engineers have tried to acquire Lunarkin specimens, hoping to utilize their buoyancy in flight experiments, but sadly, the creatures invariably deflate and die when captured.

RAKKIDA

Natural predators of Mounders, the lithe and lupine Rakkida have large, sharp teeth that protrude from their mouths even when closed. Their hairless flanks are patterned with stripes that run down the sides of their rib cages, and they have short, vestigial, bat-like wings that are unsuitable for flight. Rakkida hunt in packs, executing advanced team tactics unseen in the rest of the animal world, laying ambushes for their prey and organizing raiding parties to attack protected livestock. Midway through the Age of Division the Skeksis tried to subjugate the Rakkida, but the creatures were mostly too cunning for capture, and those that were ensnared fiercely resisted domestication. The Rakkida were a favorite quarry of skekMal the Hunter, who considered them one of the few beasts of Thra as formidable as himself.

TUMBELOTH

Notable for possessing both mammalian and reptilian features, Tumbeloth have a hard shell into which they retreat to protect their soft furry limbs and head. Denizens of the Castle of the Crystal, Tumbeloth move through the structure's catacombs using several prehensile tentacles they shoot from the sides of their shells.

Forgotten for over a hundred trine after the healing of the Crystal, Tumbeloths bred and developed in the depths of the uninhabited castle, multiplying until they were its most populous residents.

Tumbeloth are inquisitive and mischievous, with a tendency to steal items of great value and hide them away deep in the castle. If the Tumbeloth befriends another being, it will pull its shell apart with its tentacles, turning its entire body inside out to show it has nothing to hide.

ARDUFF

With sharp, lupine features, slender needle teeth, and a plumed tail that twitched and wagged when it sighted prey, the Arduff was an apex predator that dominated the Crystal Desert during the Age of Innocence.

Thra could be a frightening place during this time, long before the Gelfling tribes had developed modern methods of shelter and protection. For many trine, Gelfling were the main food source for the Arduff, who hunted at dusk, dragging victims from their rudimentary shelters. This constant threat became a driving force in the development of Gelfling civilization, forcing them to forge their first weapons and end the Arduff's domination.

By the time of the Age of Division, the long-extinct Arduff had become a creature of myth.

DAEYDOIM

Although a Daeydoim has six long, powerful legs, it moves across the sands of the Crystal Desert nearly silently, distributing its weight on wide, solid hooves that prevent it from sinking into the region's deep dunes.

The fringed, heat-reflecting dorsal scales of the Daeydoim range in color from translucent red to black and sit atop a torso blanketed with white downy fur. Though Daeydoims sport an imposing toothy maw, they are friendly, gentle creatures. Daeydoims have not been domesticated by the Dousan, but they will carry travelers through the desert for as little as a few spoons of precious water and a scratch on the snout.

FUCHSIA WORT BEETLE

Fuchsia Wort Beetles rub their hind legs together to produce a soothing lullaby that can be heard throughout the wetlands of Sog. The insects are a staple of the Drenchen diet, and children of the tribe are often tasked with collecting them by the thousands. Drenchen chefs use the Beetles' plump abdomens to create protein-rich stir-fries, along with many other dishes.

HOOYIM

Silver-gilled fish with glassy metallic scales,
Hooyim frequently come to the sea's surface in
large schools to bask in the warmth of the suns,
sparkling with enough intensity to blind passing sailors.
The "silver jewels of the Sifan," Hooyim are a prized catch and
can range in size from fingerlings that need to be thrown back,
to monsters that snap lines and chew through nets. Many a
Gelfling tale has been spun around the campfire about the
gargantuan Hooyim that got away.

MUSKI

While it resembles an eel or bottom-feeding fish, the Muski is capable of leaving its watery homes by levitation—floating or "swimming" through the air for sustained periods before landing in the marshy waters of Sog to rejuvenate. Although they feed on smaller fish and land animals, muski have been known to form strong bonds with Gelfling—in fact, juvenile muski are sometimes kept as companion animals by Drenchen.

Myrrhie & Krikid

Found in the pool that sits at the heart of the Valley of the Mystics, these rare fish were completely unknown outside of the urRu for the first three ages of Thra. Myrrhie are identifiable by their yellow and brown scales while Krikid have long, wriggling bodies and reflective blue coloration. They were later introduced to the rivers of the Endless Forest and the wetlands of Thra so that more Gelfling might enjoy their beauty.

SHROOKIL

Shrookil were six-eyed birds with long beaks and necks. They had stubby wings and could fly short distances but were mostly found pecking around the floor of the Endless Forest. While largely unremarkable, the Shrookil became legendary for its song, a startling lament only heard at the very end of its life.

Shrookil were hunted to extinction by the Skeksis early in the Age of Division, but their song lives on through Gelfling bards, who incorporate the melancholy tune into many of their ballads. The trill of the Shrookil symbolizes a good death after a life well-lived.

SWOTHEL

The Swothel is a large mammal that roams the Crystal Desert. It has four legs, all with backward-facing knees, and a short prehensile snout that it uses to scent water. When Swothel have the opportunity to hydrate, they drink more than their fill and store the rest in their hump. Swothel also produce milk. Many a weary Gelfling lost in the desert owes its life to the creature's sweet glowing milk, a gift the placid Swothel gives freely.

RUSWHA

The Ruswha is a serpentine predator with reflective green eyes and a chin that buckles under the weight of its massive underbite. Eel-like in anatomy, these amphibious pack animals work together to corner prey both in and out of water. Ruswha can be found in the marshes of Sog and the underground rivers of Grot. Luckily, they are not large enough to be a threat to Gelfling, but the aggressive creature can still deliver an extremely painful bite.

VLISTE-STABA
AND THE GREAT TREES

Vliste-Staba, the Sanctuary Tree of Grot, and the other Great Trees of Thra hold the history of the world inside their vast, brain-like root systems. They are ancient beings, some of the oldest living things on Thra, and the life-forms with the closest connection to the Crystal.

For thousands of trine, each tree watched Gelfling societies rise and grow. While they never favored the Gelfling over Thra's other inhabitants, the Great Trees were a constant source of guidance and inspiration for the seven clans. During the Age of Division, the Sanctuary Tree became the first to sense the threat posed by the Skeksis and the Darkening.

Vliste-Staba died during the Age of Resistance, but before passing, it imparted its world-healing powers on the Gelfling hero, Deet. But such powers came at a price . . .

TITAN BOOKS

144 Southwark Street
London SE1 0UP
www.titanbooks.com

 Find us on Facebook: www.facebook.com/titanbooks

Follow us on Twitter: @TitanBooks

The Dark Crystal: Age of Resistance © 2019 Netflix, Inc.

© 1982, 2020 The Jim Henson Company. JIM HENSON's mark &
logo, THE DARK CRYSTAL mark & logo, characters and elements
are trademarks of The Jim Henson Company. All Rights Reserved.

Published by Titan Books, London, in 2020.

No part of this book may be reproduced, stored in a retrieval
system, or transmitted, in any form or by any means without
the prior written permission of the publisher, nor be otherwise
circulated in any form of binding or cover other than that in
which it is published and without a similar condition being
imposed on the subsequent publisher.

Published by arrangement with Insight Editions,
PO Box 3088, San Rafael, CA, 94912, USA.
www.insighteditions.com

A CIP Catalogue record for this title is available from
the British Library.

ISBN: 978-1-78909-620-0

Publisher: Raoul Goff
Associate Publisher: Vanessa Lopez
Creative Director: Chrissy Kwasnik
VP of Manufacturing: Alix Nicholaeff
Designer: Amy DeGrote
Executive Editor: Chris Prince
Editorial Assistant: Harrison Tunggal
Managing Editor: Lauren LePera
Senior Production Editor: Elaine Ou
Production Director/Subsidiary Rights: Lina s Palma
Senior Production Manager: Greg Steffen

Illustrations by Iris Compiet

Moog created by Yukari Masuike, winner of the Design a
New Creature for *The Dark Crystal: Age of Resistance* contest.

ROOTS of PEACE   REPLANTED PAPER

Manufactured in China by Insight Editions

10 9 8 7 6 5 4 3 2

INSIGHT EDITIONS would like to thank everyone at
the Jim Henson Company that made this book possible,
including Lisa Henson, Jim Formanek, Nicole Goldman,
Rita Peruggi, Tim O'Brien, Carla DellaVedova, Shannon
Robles, Karen Falk, and Susie Tofte.

ADAM CESARE would like to thank Jeffrey Addis
and Will Matthews for their encouragement, guidance,
and insights from the *Dark Crystal: Age of Resistance*
writers' room. Allyson Gronowitz and Matthew Levine
at BOOM! Studios for helping him navigate the world
of Thra the first time. Chris Prince for his patience and
knowledge. Frank Oz, Brian and Wendy Froud, Jim
Henson, and everyone who made the original film.
And his beloved wife, Jen.

IRIS COMPIET would like to thank Brian and Wendy
Froud, not only for breathing life into the creatures of
Thra but also for providing the opportunity to join in
the discovery of these wonderful beings brought to life
by the amazing team at the Jim Henson Company. At
Insight Editions, Chris Prince, Chrissy Kwasnik, and
Amy DeGrote for the wonderful collaboration. And
finally, her husband, Bart, for the moral support.